Tirio Maders

ALEXANDRIA:

A HISTORY AND A GUIDE

EDWARD MORGAN FORSTER was born on January 1, 1879, and educated at Tonbridge School and King's College, Cambridge. He lived in Italy from 1905 to 1907, where he wrote his first novels, including *A Room with a View*, published in 1908. *Howard's End* (1910) marked his return to England, and a year later he made the first of two visits to India. His most famous novel, *A Passage to India*, was the fruit of his visits there. Published in 1924, it was awarded the Femina Vie Heureuse and James Tait Black Memorial prizes, and the stage adaptation of this novel opened for a successful run in London in 1960. In 1937 E. M. Forster was awarded the Benson Medal of the Royal Society of Literature, and in 1953 he was made a Member of the Order of the British Empire. He is an honorary fellow of nine universities, including Oxford, Cambridge, and Hamilton College, U.S.A.

Vue d'Alexandrie extraite du

JOVRNAL

DES VOYAGES

DE MONSIEVR

DE MONCONYS

LYON MDCLXV

———

See p. 89.

ALEXANDRIA:

A HISTORY AND A GUIDE

BY

E. M. FORSTER

If a man make a pilgrimage round Alexandria in the morning, God will make for him a golden crown, set with pearls, perfumed with musk and camphor, and shining from the East to the West.
                                    Ibn Dukmak.

To any vision must be brought an eye adapted to what is to be seen.
                                    Plotinus.

Anchor Books
Doubleday & Company, Inc.
Garden City, New York
1961

COVER DESIGN BY ROBIN JACQUES
TYPOGRAPHY BY SUSAN SIEN

Library of Congress Catalog Card Number 61–7648
Copyright © 1961 by Edward Morgan Forster
Printed in the United States of America

To G. H. L.

CONTENTS

PART II: GUIDE

SECTION I: FROM THE SQUARE TO THE RUE ROSETTE

INTRODUCTION TO THE NEW EDITION

There have already been two editions of this little book. Here is the third, and here is my opportunity of unfolding a slight but complicated tale.

The text of the first edition (the one here reproduced) was written by me during the First World War when I was stationed in Alexandria as the result of volunteering for the Red Cross. I arrived there in the autumn of 1915 in a slightly heroic mood. A Turkish invasion was threatened, and although a civilian I might find myself in the battle line. The threat passed and my mood changed. What had begun as an outpost turned into something suspiciously like a funk-hole, and I stuck in it for over three years, visiting hospitals, collecting information, and writing reports. "You are such a wonderful *sticker*," a detestable Red Cross colonel once said to me scathingly. I was; and I dared not retort that it takes both stickers and climbers to make a world.

I was dressed like a sort of officer myself, but allowed to take the things off between whiles, and it was thus that I apprehended the magic and the antiquity and the complexity of the city, and determined to write about her. A guidebook suggested itself. I have always respected guidebooks—particularly the earlier Baedekers and Murrays—and I tried to work in some history as well, by a technique explained on p. xix. My friends encouraged me—English, Greek, American, French, Italian, Norwegian, Syrian, Egyptian were then among them, for I had inserted myself a little into Levantine life. And visions kept coming as I went about in trams or on foot or bathed in the delicious sea. For instance, I would multiply the height of the Fort of Kait Bey by four and so envisage the Pharos which had once stood on the same site. At the crossing of the two main streets I would erect the tomb of Alexander the Great. I would follow Alexander in imagination to Siwa, the oasis of Jupiter Amnon, where he was saluted as the Son of God. And I would follow the monks too, to the desolate Wady Natrum when they burst to murder Hypatia.

Which was all very well; but how was one to get published?

Here a piece of amazing good fortune befell me.

There is, or rather was, in the Rue Chérif Pacha (if it is still called that) an unobtrusive-looking shop. It sold stationery. But it was actually the Alexandria branch of an important London printing firm—Messrs. Whitehead Morris of Tower Hill. The local manager, Mr. Mann, heard of my project and was interested in it, though it lay outside his normal work. There were many delays and some differences of opinion, but it duly came out after the war and after my return to England, in 1922.

Shortly after publication a disaster occurred. As the result of a fire in the storerooms nearly the whole of the edition was destroyed. That is why copies of it are so rare.

It was a sad setback, and a few years later as I was passing through Alexandria, on my way back from South Africa, I actually lost my way as I came out of its new Railway Station. What a humiliating experience for the writer of a Guide! I could not even find

my way about my own city! It seemed to me that a
new edition was called for, although there was not
then any audible call, and although I could not under-
take the work of revision. But in one respect Alexandria
had not changed; she was still the city of friends who
were willing unselfishly to set aside their own work
and to work for others. They brought the "guide" part
of the book up to date by visiting all the sites and objects mentioned, and they corrected my worst blunders
in the "history" part. This edition came out in 1938,
again under the auspices of the Alexandria branch of
Messrs. Whitehead Morris. It did not sell well, perhaps
because the Second World War started next year.
Copies of it are rare. The friends in question once suggested a new (local) edition, and pointed out that certain alterations must be made, or the book would
offend Egyptian national suceptibilities. I bet it would.
There are scarcely any national susceptibilities it does
not offend. The only locality it shouldn't offend is
Alexandria herself, who in the 2,000 years of her life
has never taken national susceptibilities too seriously.

And this brings me to Cavafy. One of the joys of
those years was my friendship with the great Greek
poet who so poignantly conveys the civilisation of his
chosen city. C. P. Cavafy was not then widely known
and the translation of "The God Abandons Antony"
(p. 104) by our friend George Valassopoulo represents
his first appearance in English. He has been fully
translated since, and widely eulogised—for instance by
a later lover of Alexandria, Mr. Lawrence Durrell. I
dedicated the second edition of this book to Cavafy
after his death.

The first edition was dedicated to G. H. Ludolf, another of the many who helped me.

The present edition appears through the courtesy of

Messrs. Walter & Whitehead, Ltd., the representatives
of Messrs. Whitehead Morris.

Finally: this is not my only tribute to Alexandria.
There is also *Pharos and Pharillon,* a volume of essays,
published in 1923 by Messrs. A. Knopf in the United
States and by the Hogarth Press in England.

E. M. Forster
Cambridge, England. 1960

PREFACE

This book consists of two parts: a History and a Guide.

The "History" attempts (after the fashion of a pageant) to marshal the activities of Alexandria during the two thousand two hundred and fifty years of her existence. Starting with the heroic figure of Alexander the Great, it inspects the dynasty of the Ptolemies, and in particular the career of the last of them, Cleopatra; an account of Ptolemaic literature and science follows, and closes this splendid period, to which I have given the title of "Greco-Egyptian." The second period, called "Christian," begins with the rule of Rome, and traces the fortunes of Christianity, first as a persecuted and then as a persecuting power: all is lost in 641, when the Patriarch Cyrus betrays Alexandria to the Arabs. An interlude comes next—"The Spiritual City"—which meditates upon Alexandrian philosophy and religion, both Pagan and Christian: it seemed better to segregate these subjects, partly because they interrupt the main historical procession, partly because many readers are not interested in them. History is resumed in the "Arab Period," which is of no importance though it lasts over 1,000 years—from Amr to Napoleon. With Napoleon begins the "Modern Period," the main feature of which is the building of the city we now see under the auspices of Mohammed Ali: and the pageant concludes, as well as it may, with an account of the events of 1882, and with surmises as to future municipal developments.

The "History" is written in short sections, and at the end of each section are references to the second part—the "Guide." *On these references the chief utility of the book depends,* so the reader is begged to take special note of them: they may help him to link the present and the past. Suppose, for instance, he has read in the History about the Pharos: at the end of the section he will find references to Fort Kait Bey where the Pharos stood, to Abousir where there is a miniature replica of it, and to the Coin Room in the Museum, where it appears on the moneys of Domitian and Hadrian. Or again, suppose that the tragic fate of Hypatia has touched him: at the end will be references to the Caesareum, where Hypatia was murdered, and to the Wady Natrun, where the monks who murdered her generally resided. Or the British victories of 1801: he will be referred to the country over which our troops marched, to the Abercrombie Monument at Sidi Gaber, and to a tombstone in the courtyard of the Greek Patriarchate. The "sights" of Alexandria are in themselves not interesting, but they fascinate when we approach them through the past, and this is what I have tried to do by the double arrangement of History and Guide.

The "Guide" calls for no introduction. It is written from the practical standpoint, and is intended to be used on the spot. Maps and plans accompany it. The city is divided into sections, the visitor in every case starting from the Square. Other sections deal with the environs, and with the surrounding country as far as Rosetta on the east and Abousir on the west. In transliterating Arabic names I have preferred the French system: there are three English systems, each backed by a rival government department, so the French seems the safer course, and if I have not kept to it rigidly, I am only following, though at a respectful distance, the example of the Alexandria Municipality. Here and there some History has crept into the Guide—notably in the case of Aboukir, whose fortunes, though dependent on Alexandria's, present features of their own.

AUTHORITIES

There is, so far as I know, no monograph on Alexandria, and though the present little book makes no claim to original research, it has drawn together much information that was hitherto scattered. The following works, among others, have been consulted: those marked with an asterisk are published locally.

(A). HISTORY:—

Ptolemaic Period:— *Bouché-Leclercq, Histoire des Lagides.* A scholarly and delightful work. 4 vols.

Ptolemaic Literature:—*A. Couat, La Poésie Alex-andrine;* well written. *Theocritus,* translated A. Lang.

Christian Period:— No satisfactory work. S. *Sharpe, History of Egypt until the Arab Conquest,* vol. 2 may be consulted; also *Gibbon,* chs. 21 and 47. *Mrs. Butcher, The Story of the Church in Egypt* is full of information, but uncritical and diffuse.

Arab Conquest:—*A. J. Butler, The Arab Conquest of Egypt.* A monograph of the highest merit, brilliantly written and practically reconstructing the episode.

Jewish Thought:—*E. Herriot, Philon le Juif.*

Neo-Platonism:—Various works. There is a lucid introduction to Plotinus in S. *McKenna, Translation of the Enneads,* vol. 1; this admirable translation is still in progress. *Porphyry's Letter to Marcella* (translated, A. Gardner) is also interesting.

Christian Theology:—See under "Christian Period." The Fathers can be read in the *Ante-Nicene Christian Library*.

Arab Period:—Too obscure to possess a history.

Napoleonic Wars:—*Mahan, Influence of Sea Power upon the French Revolution*, chs. 9 and 10. R. T. Wilson, *History of the British Expedition to Egypt*. See also below, under Aboukir.

General Modern History:—*D. A. Cameron, Egypt in the Nineteenth Century*. A well-written book by the late Consul General at Alexandria; contains good account of Mohammed Ali. The works of Lord Cromer, W. S. Blunt and Sir V. Chirol are also useful.

Events of 1882:—*C. Royle, The Egyptian Campaigns*.

One or two novels and plays dealing with the History may here be mentioned. The career of Cleopatra has inspired two noble tragedies, Shakespeare's *Antony and Cleopatra*, and Dryden's *All for Love;* extracts from them are given on p. 231. Dryden's masterpiece should be better known; it is most moving, admirably constructed, and contains some magnificent scenes. A novel by Pierre Loüys, *Aphrodite*, also treats of the period, but in a scented Parisian way.—Anatole France, *Thaïs*, pictures life in the 4th cent. A.D.; the details are both vivid and accurate, and build up a perfect work of art.—For the early 5th cent. there is Charles Kingsley's *Hypatia*, a rousing yarn about the final contest between Paganism and Christianity; Kingsley is always readable, but his bluff burly mind was incapable of understanding Alexandria.—Two good novels by Marmaduke Pickthall, *Said the Fisherman* and *Children of the Nile* touch upon events in the modern period.

(B). GUIDE:—

*E. Breccia, Alexandrea ad Aegyptum. In French: English translation announced. Deals mainly with Classical Antiquities. Two sections— the first dealing with the remains in the city and environs, the second with the Greco-Roman Museum, of which Professor Breccia is the distinguished Curator. I am under much obligation to this fine scholarly book, especially in the following sections:—Greco-Roman Museum, Catacombs of Anfouchi and Kom es Chogafa, Serapeum, Abousir.

Prehistoric Harbour:—*E. Jondet, Les Ports submergés de l'ancienne Isle de Pharos. A monograph by the discoverer. Magnificent Maps.

Pharos and Fort Kait Bey:—H. Thiersch, Pharos, antike Islam und Occident. A standard monograph, but exhibiting the defects as well as the merits of German Scholarship.

Canopus and Aboukir:—*J. Faivre, Canopus, Menouthis, Aboukir. Published in French and English. *R. D. Downes, A History of Canopus. These excellent pamphlets supplement one another, the first dealing with the literary evidence, the second with the typography.

Rosetta:—*Max Herz Bey, Les Mosquées de Rosette (various articles in the Comptes Rendus of the Comité de Conservation des Monuments Arabes).

St. Menas:—*C. M. Koufmann, La Decouverte des Sanctuaires de Menas. By the Excavator.

Natrun Monasteries:—A. J. Butler, Ancient Coptic Churches.

Many friends have also helped me, among whom I would particularly thank the following:—Mr. George Antonius for his assistance with those interesting but little known buildings, the Alexandria Mosques; Mr.

M. S. Briggs for his help in the Rosetta section; Dr. A. J. Butler for permission to reproduce two plans of the Natrun Churches; Mr. C. P. Cavafy for permission to publish one of his poems, and Mr. G. Valassopoulo for translating the same; the Rev. R. D. Downes for his help at Aboukir; Mr. R. A. Furness for his verse translations from Callimachus and other Greek poets; M. E. Jondet, Director of Ports and Lights, for taking me to see his fascinating discovery, the Prehistoric Harbour, and for placing at my disposal his unrivalled collection of Maps and Views, two of which I have reproduced; and above all Mr. G. H. Ludolf, to whose suggestion this book is due, and without whose help it would never have been completed. I shall never forget the kindness that I have received at Alexandria, and in no wise endorse the verdict of my predecessor the poet Gelal ed Din ben Mokram who monstrously asserts that:—

> The visitor to Alexandria receives nothing in the way
>   of hospitality
> Except some water and an account of Pompey's
>   Pillar.
> Those who wish to treat him very well go so far as to
>   offer some fresh air
> And to tell him where the Lighthouse is.
> They also instruct him about the sea and its waves,
> Adding a description of the large Greek boats.
> The visitor need not aspire to receive any bread,
> For to a request of this sort there is no reply.

Circumstances which I could not control have delayed the publication of the book, but, with the help of friends, I have tried to bring the "Guide" up to date as far as possible.

PART I
HISTORY

MEDITERRANEAN SEA

Anfouchi Tombs

PREHISTORIC HARBOUR

Military Hospital

RUE RAS EL TIN

Ras el Tin Palace

Breakwater

Lighthouse

WESTERN HARBOUR
(EUNOSTOS)

Franciscan Ch.

MINET EL BASSAL

to Mex

GABBARI

Kom es Chogafa

Fishing Village

to Mex & the Western Desert

Plan of
ALEXANDRIA

LAKE MARIOUT

SECTION I

Greco-Egyptian Period

THE LAND AND THE WATERS

The situation of Alexandria is most curious. To understand it we must go back many thousand years.

Ages ago, before there was civilisation in Egypt, or the delta of the Nile had been formed, the whole of the country as far south as Cairo lay under the sea. The shores of this sea were a limestone desert. The coastline was smooth as a rule, but at the north-west corner an extraordinary spur jutted out from the main mass. It was not more than a mile wide, but many miles long. Its base is not far from the modern Bahig. Alexandria is built half-way down it, and its tip is the headland of Aboukir. On each side of it there used to be deep salt water.

Centuries passed, and the Nile, issuing out of his crack above Cairo, kept carrying down the muds of Upper Egypt, and dropping them as soon as his current slackened. In the north-west corner they were arrested by this spur, and began to silt up against it. It was a shelter not only from the outer sea, but from the prevalent wind. Alluvial land appeared; the huge shallow lake of Mariout was formed; and the current of the Nile, unable to escape through the limestone barrier, rounded the headland of Aboukir, and entered the outer sea by what was known in historical times as the "Canopic" Mouth.

This explains one characteristic of Alexandrian scenery—the long narrow ridge edged on the north by the sea and on the south by a lake and flat fields. But it does not explain why Alexandria has a harbour.

To the north of the spur, and more or less parallel to it, runs a second limestone range. It is much shorter than the spur and much lower, being often below the surface of the sea in the form of reefs. It seems unimportant. But without it there would have been no harbour (and consequently no town), because it breaks the force of the waves. Starting at Agame it continues as a series of rocks across the entrance of the modern harbour. Then it re-emerges to form the hammer-headed promontory of Ras-el-Tin, disappears into a second series of rocks that close the entrance of the Eastern Harbour, and makes its final appearance at the promontory of Silsileh, after which it rejoins the big spur.

Such are the main features of the situation; a limestone ridge, with harbours on one side of it, and alluvial country on the other. It is a situation unique in Egypt, and the Alexandrians have never been truly Egyptian.

BEST SURVEY POINTS ON RIDGE ARE:

    QUARRIES BEYOND MEX: p. 185.
    HILL OF ABOU EL NAWATIR: p. 180.
    MONTAZAH: p. 186.
    HEADLAND OF ABOUKIR: p. 196.

PHAROS, RHAKOTIS, CANOPUS

Who first settled on this remarkable stretch of coast? There seem to have been three early centres.

(i)   Homer (Odyssey, Book iv) says:—

"There is an island in the surging sea, which they call Pharos, lying off Egypt. It has a harbour with good anchorage, and hence they put out to sea after drawing water."

Homer's island is now the promontory of Ras-el-Tin; the intervening channel has silted up. There are no traces of any early settlement on its soil, but in the sea to its north and west the masonry of a prehistoric harbour has been found. Homer goes on to tell how Menelaus was becalmed on Pharos as he returned from Troy, and how he could not get away until he had entrapped Proteus, the divine king of the island, and exacted a favourable wind. A similar legend has been found in an ancient Egyptian papyrus. There the King is called the "Prouti" or "Pharaoh." "Prouti" is probably the original of Homer's "Proteus," "Pharaoh" of his "Pharos." It is significant that our first glimpse of the coast should be through the eyes of a Greek sailor.

(ii) But our historical survey must begin with Rhakotis. Rhakotis was a small Egyptian town built on the rise where "Pompey's Pillar" stands now, and it existed as long ago as 1,300 B.C., for statues of that time have been found here. The people were coast-guards and goat herds. Their chief god was Osiris. Rhakotis was never important in itself. But it is important as an element in the great Greek city that was built up round it. It was a little lump of Egypt. Compare it to the Arab villages and slums that have been embedded in the scheme of the modern town—to Mazarita or to Kom-el-Dik. Rhakotis was like one of these. The native and conservative element naturally rallied to it, and it became the site for Alexandria's great religious effort— the cult of Serapis.

(iii) At the tip of the limestone ridge, where the Nile once entered the sea, was another early settlement. It also appears in Greek legend. In historical times, it was known as Canopus.

ALEXANDER THE GREAT (B.C. 331)

Few cities have made so magnificent an entry into history as Alexandria. She was founded by Alexander the Great.

When he arrived here he was only twenty-five years old. His career must be sketched. He was a Macedonian and had begun by destroying the city-civilisation of ancient Greece. But he did not hate the Greeks, no, he admired them immensely and desired to be treated as if he was one, and his next exploit was to lead a crusade against Greece's traditional enemy, Persia, and to defeat her in two tremendous battles, one at the Dardanelles and one in Asia Minor. As soon as he conquered Syria, Egypt fell into his hands, and fell willingly, for she too hated the Persians. He went to Memphis (near modern Cairo). Then he descended the Nile to the coast, and ordered his architect Dinocrates to build round the nucleus of Rhakotis a magnificent Greek city. This was not mere idealism on his part, or rather idealism was happily combined with utility. He needed a capital for his new Egyptian kingdom, and to link it with Macedonia that capital had to be on the coast. Here was the very place—a splendid harbour, a perfect climate, fresh water, limestone quarries, and easy access to the Nile. Here he would perpetuate all that was best in Hellenism, and would create a metropolis for that greater Greece that should consist not of city-states but of kingdoms, and should include the whole inhabited world.

Alexandria was founded.

Having given his orders, the young man hurried on. He never saw a single building rise. His next care was a visit to the temple of Ammon in the Siwan Oasis, where the priest saluted him as a god, and henceforward his Greek sympathies declined. He became an Oriental, a cosmopolitan almost, and though he fought Persia again, it was in a new spirit. He wanted to harmonise the world now, not to Hellenise it, and must have looked back on Alexandria as a creation of his immaturity. But he was after all to return to her. Eight years later, having conquered Persia, he died, and his body, after some vicissitudes, was brought to Memphis for burial. The High Priest refused to receive it there. "Do not settle him here," he cried, "but at the city he has built at Rhakotis, for wherever this body must lie the city will be uneasy, disturbed with wars and battles." So he descended the Nile again, wrapped in gold and enclosed in a coffin of glass, and he was buried at the centre of Alexandria, by her great cross roads, to be her civic hero and tutelary god.

COIN OF ALEXANDER: Museum, Room 3.
STATUES OF HIM: Museum, Rooms 12, 16.
HIS TOMB (Soma): p. 112.
TOMBSTONE OF MACEDONIAN OFFICER: Museum,
  Room 20.

THE FOUNDATION PLAN
(*See Map of Ancient City p.* 106)

Before dissecting Alexander's plan we must remember three differences in the configuration of the soil as it existed in his day.

(i)   As already pointed out, Ras-el-Tin was then an island. He thought of building here, but rejected the site as too cramped. A shrine to his dead friend Hephaestion rose here, that was all.

(ii)   Lake Mariout was much deeper then than now, and directly connected with the Nile. Consequently it was almost as important a water-way as the sea, and a lake harbour was an integral part of the plan.

(iii)   There was then through water-connection between the Mediterranean and the Red Sea. The ancient Egyptians had cut a canal from the Nile at Memphis down to the salt lakes that begin by the modern Ismailia. Thus Alexandria stood in the position of Port Said to-day; a maritime gate-way to India and the remoter east.

The city was oblong, and filled up the strip between the lake and the sea; she was laid out in rigidly straight lines. Her main street (the "Canopic") still exists in part as the Rue Rosette. It ran almost due east and west—a bad direction because it was cut off from the cool north wind that is the real tutelary god of Alexandria, but, owing to the site, nothing else could be contrived. Westward it terminated in the sea; eastward it proceeded to Canopus (Aboukir). It was the natural highway along the limestone spur, and no doubt existed long before Alexander came.

Crossing the Canopic Street, and following the line of the present Rue Nebi Daniel, was the second main artery, the street of the Soma. It started at the Lake Harbour and ran northward to the sea. Where it intersected the Canopic Street stood the Soma, or burial place of Alexander—close to the present Mosque. Parallel to these two streets ran others, dividing the city into blocks of an American regularity. It could not have been picturesque, but the Greeks did not desire picturesqueness. They liked to lay their towns out evenly —Rhodes and Halicarnassus had just been laid out on the same lines—and the only natural feature they cared to utilise was the sea. The blocks were labelled according to the letters of the Greek alphabet.

Of the sea front magnificent use was to be made. Only one feature shall be mentioned here: the dyke Heptastadion (seven stades long) which was built to connect the island of Pharos and the mainland. It performed two functions; it enlarged the city area, and it broke the force of the currents and created a double harbour—the Great Harbour to the east and the Eunostos ("Safe Return") to the west. In the Arab period the Heptastadion silted up and became the neck of land that leads to Ras-el-Tin.

The course of the walls is uncertain. Perhaps their eastern course was from the promontory of Silsileh to the lake, and their western from the modern Gabbari to the lake. Their foundations were accompanied by a portent of the usual type. There was not enough chalk to mark the outlines, so meal had to be substituted, and a number of birds flew out of the lake and ate it all up. The Greeks interpreted the portent satisfactorily: to the Egyptians it might well have symbolised

the advent of the hungry foreigner. We are not told
what was substituted for the meal, but somehow or
other the walls were built and were studded at fre-
quent intervals with towers.

THE FIRST THREE PTOLEMIES

PTOLEMY I., SOTER, 323–285.
PTOLEMY II., PHILADELPHUS, 285–247.
PTOLEMY III., EUERGETES, 247–222.

(*See Genealogical Tree p.* 14)

When Alexander died the empire was divided among his generals, who ruled for a little in the name of his half-brother or of his son, but who soon proclaimed themselves as independent kings. Egypt fell to the ablest and most discreet of these generals, a Macedonian named Ptolemy. Ptolemy was no soaring idealist. He desired neither to Hellenise the world nor to harmonise it. But he was no cynic either. He respected mental as well as material activity. He had been present at the foundation of Alexandria, and had evidently decided that the place would suit him, and now, taking up his abode in the unfinished city, he began to adorn her with architecture and scholarship and song. Rival generals, especially in Asia Minor and Macedonia, occupied much of his energy. At the very beginning of his rule he was involved in a curious war for the possession of the corpse of Alexander, which he had kidnapped as it was on its way from Persia to the Oasis of Ammon. Ptolemy annexed the corpse and much else. Before he died he had assumed the titles of King and of Soter (saviour), and had added to his kingdom Cyrene, Palestine, Cyprus, and parts of the Asia Minor coast. Of this substantial domain Alexandria was the capital, and also the geographic centre. Then, as now, she belonged not so much to Egypt as to the Mediterranean, and the Ptolemies realised this. Up in Egypt

GENEALOGICAL TREE OF THE PTOLEMIES

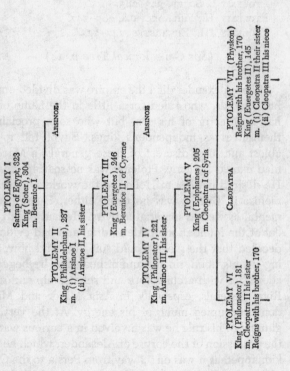

PTOLEMY I
Satrap of Egypt, 323
King (Soter), 304
m. Berenice I

ARSINOE,

PTOLEMY II
King (Philadelphus), 287
m. (i) Arsinoe I
   (ii) Arsinoe II, his sister

PTOLEMY III
King (Euergetes), 246
m. Berenice II, of Cyrene

ARSINOE,

PTOLEMY IV
King (Philopator), 221
m. Arsinoe III, his sister

PTOLEMY V
King (Epiphanes), 205
m. Cleopatra I of Syria

CLEOPATRA

PTOLEMY VI
King (Philometor) 181
m. Cleopatra II his sister
Reigns with his brother, 170

PTOLEMY VII (Physkon)
Reigns with his brother, 170
King (Euergetes II), 145
m. (i) Cleopatra II their sister
   (ii) Cleopatra III his niece

PTOLEMY VIII
King (Eupator) 145.
d. same year

CLEOPATRA

CLEOPATRA

PTOLEMY X* (Lathyrus)
King (Soter II) 116
Expelled to Cyprus 108-88
m. his sister Cleopatra IV
d. 80

(illegitimate)
PTOLEMY XIII (Auletes)
King (Neos Dionyus) 80
m. his sister Cleopatra V
banished 58-55 d. 51

Cleopatra-Berenice

BERENICE IV
Queen 58-55

CLEOPATRA VI (Philopator) 51-47
m. her brothers Ptolemy XIV & XV (48-44)
mistress of Julius Caesar (48-30)
and of M. Antony (40-30)

PTOLEMY XVI (Caesarion)
(son by Caesar)
44-30

PTOLEMY XII
King (Alexander I) 108-88
m. (i) ?
    (ii) his niece, Cleopatra
    Berenice III

PTOLEMY XI
King (Alexander II) 80
m. his stepmother and cousin
Cleopatra-Berenice III
End of Legitimate branch

PTOLEMY XV
47-44

PTOLEMY XIV
51-30

ARSINOE

*Ptolemy IX is omitted from this list; he was probably a dead son of Ptolemy VII and Cleopatra II, whom they inserted posthumously in the annals as "Neos Philopator."

they played the Pharaoh, and built solemn archaistic temples like Edfu and Kom Ombo. Down in Alexandria they were Hellenistic.

The second Ptolemy, Philadelphus, (Friend of his Sister), was a more pretentious person than his father. He is famous through the praises of the poets whom he patronised and of the Jews whom he invited, but his personal achievements were slight. Indeed the chief event of his reign is domestic rather than military—in 277 he married his sister Arsinoe. This was as startling to Greek feelings as it is to Christian, but in Egypt he had a prototype in the god Osiris who had married his sister Isis, and he justified the union on the highest sacerdotal grounds. He and Arsinoe were deified as the "Adelphian Gods," in whose equal veins flowed the uncontaminated blood of their divine father, the general, and their example was followed, when possible, by their successors. It was the pride of race carried to an extreme degree. The royalties of to-day, for fear of debasing their stock, marry first cousins; the Ptolemies, more logical, tried to propagate within even narrower limits. In flesh, as in spirit, the dynasty claimed to be apart from common men, and to appear as successive emanations of the Deity, in pairs of male and female. Arsinoe—to come back to earth—was a domineering and sinister woman. She was seven years older than her brother, and when they married he had already a wife, whom she drove from Alexandria by her intrigues. However, he liked her and when, a martyr to indigestion, she died, he was so far inconsolable that he did not marry again.

The closing years of his reign were divided between his mistresses and the gout. During a respite from the latter he looked out of his palace window on some public holiday, and saw beneath him the natives picnicking on the sand, as they do at the feast of Shem-el-Nessem to-day. They were obscure, they were happy. "Why can I not be like them?" sighed the old king, and burst into tears. His reign had been imposing rather than beautiful and had initiated little in Alexandrian civilisation beyond the somewhat equivocal item of a mystic marriage. He could endow and patronise. But, unlike Alexander, unlike his father, he could not create. He completed what they had laid down, and appropriated the praise.

Ptolemy Euergetes (Well-doer) was the son of Philadelphus by his first wife. In character he resembled his grandfather. He was a sensible and successful soldier, with a taste for science. By marrying his cousin Berenice, he secured Cyrene which had lapsed—Berenice the most highly praised of all the Ptolemaic Queens, though we know nothing of her character. In their reign the power of Egypt and the splendour of Alexandria came to their height. It is now time to examine that splendour. One hundred years have passed since Alexander laid the foundations. What has been built upon them?

COINS OF FIRST THREE PTOLEMIES: Museum, Room 3.
INSCRIPTIONS: Museum, Rooms 6, 22.
PTOLEMY EUERGETES, STATUES: Museum, Room 12.
BERENICE, STATUES: Museum, Rooms 4, 12.

THE PTOLEMAIC CITY
(*See Map of Ancient City p.* 106)

The following were the most important buildings in the Ptolemaic city.

(i). THE LIGHTHOUSE.
The Egyptian coast, being mainly alluvial, is difficult

to sight from the sea. It was therefore imperative to indicate, by some great monument, where the new city stood. It was desirable too to provide a guide for sailors through the limestone reefs that line the shore. For these reasons the Ptolemies built a lighthouse over four hundred feet high on the Eastern end of Pharos Island (present Fort Kait Bey). Full details are given later (p. 144); here it is enough to note that the Pharos (as it was called) was the greatest practical achievement of the Alexandrian mind and the outward expression of the mathematical studies carried on in the Mouseion; Sostratus, its architect, was contemporary with Eratosthenes and Euclid.

A fortress as well as a beacon, the Pharos was the pivot of the city's naval defences. It dominated both the harbours, and kept special watch over the more precious of them—the Eastern, which held the Royal fleet. Here the promontory of the Palace stretched towards it. Westward, it could signal over the other harbour to the Chersonese (present Fort Agame). And further west, the system was prolonged into a long line of watch towers and beacons that studded the north African coast, and connected Egypt with her daughter kingdom of Cyrene. One of these towers (that at Abousir) still remains, and shows in miniature what the Pharos must once have been.

Fort Kait Bey (Pharos): p. 144.
Coins illustrating Pharos: Museum, Room 2.
Tower of Abousir: p. 207.

(ii). The Palace.

We can locate one point in the Palace, or rather palace-system: it certainly covered the Promontory of Silsileh, which was then both longer and broader than now. But no one knows how far the buildings stretched inland, or along the shore, nor what the architecture was. Each Ptolemy made additions, and the whole formed a special quarter, somewhat like the Imperial City at Pekin. Egypt being an autocracy, the Palace was the seat of government as well as royal residence; clerks had their offices there. There was a palace-harbour (left of Silsileh), and an Island Palace or Kiosk called Antirrhodus, which rivalled the glories of Rhodes; Antirrhodus lay in the Eastern Harbour, and rocks, now deep below the surface of the sea, have been identified with it.

Inland, the Palace connected with another great system—that of the Mouseion. On its seaward side, it was prolonged by breakwaters towards the Pharos.

SILSILEH (Site of Palace): p. 178.
COLUMNS FROM LOCALITY: Museum, Room 16.

(iii). THE MOUSEION.

The Mouseion at Alexandria was the great intellectual achievement of the dynasty. Not only did it mould the literature and science of its day, but it has left a permanent impress upon thought. Its buildings have all disappeared, and the very site is conjectural; perhaps it had a façade opposite the Soma, west of the present Rue Nebi Daniel. In its vast areas were lecture halls, laboratories, observatories, a library, a dining hall, a park, and a zoo.

It was founded by Ptolemy Soter, who summoned a follower of Aristotle, Demetrius Phalerus, and ordered him to organise an institution on the lines of the Athenian Mouseion—a philosophic establishment that had contained the library of Aristotle. But the Alexandrian Mouseion soon diverged widely from its model. It was far richer and larger for one thing; the funds being administered by a priest who was appointed by the King. And it was essentially a court institution, under palace control, and knew both the advantages and disadvantages of royal patronage. In some ways it resembled a modern university, but the scholars and scientists and literary men whom it supported were under no obligation to teach; they had only to pursue their studies to the greater glory of the Ptolemies.

The most famous element in this enormous institution was the Library—sometimes called the "Mother" library to distinguish it from a later and even greater collection. 500,000 books, and a catalogue that occupied 120. The post of "Librarian" was of immense importance and its holder was the chief official in the Mouseion.

The actual literary and scientific output of the Mouseion will be considered elsewhere (p. 31).

Rue Nebi Daniel (Site of Mouseion ?): p. 112.

(iv). The Temple of Serapis.

The idea that one religion is false and another true is essentially Christian, and had not occurred to the Egyptians and Greeks who were living together at Alexandria. Each worshipped his own gods, just as he spoke his own language, but he never thought that the gods of his neighbour had no existence, and he was willing to believe that they might be his own gods under another name. The Greeks in particular held this view and had already identified Osiris, god of the world beyond death, with their Dionysus, who was a god of mysteries and also of wine. So when Ptolemy Soter decided to compound a god for his new city, he was only taking advantage of this tendency, and giving a local habitation and a name and a statue to sentiments that already existed.

Osiris was the main ingredient. He was already worshipped on the hill of Rhakotis, and he was the most celebrated of the Egyptian deities. To him was added the bull god Apis, of Memphis, whose cult had been recently revived, and out of their names was formed the compound, "Serapis." But while the origins and title of the new god were Egyptian, his appearance and attributes were Greek. His statue—ascribed to the Greek sculptor Bryaxis—showed him seated in Greek garments upon a classic throne. His features were those of the bearded Zeus, but softened and benign; indeed he more closely resembled Aesculapius, god of Healing, to whom in a civilised age men naturally turned. The basket on his head showed that he was a harvest god, the three-headed Cerberus stood by his side to show that he represented Pluto, god of the underworld.

The Ptolemies could launch such a being without any fear of wounding religious susceptibilities. What they could not have foreseen was his success. Serapis not only fulfilled their immediate political aim of providing the Alexandrians with a common cult. He spread beyond the city, beyond Egypt, and shrines to him arose all over the Mediterranean world. Osiris-Apis-Dionysus-Zeus-Aesculapius-Pluto may seem to us an artificial compound, but it stood the test of time, it satisfied men's desires, and was to be the last stronghold of Paganism against Christianity.

The Temple stood on the old citadel of Rhakotis, where "Pompey's Pillar" rises to-day. It was in the midst of a cloister, and colonnades connected it with each of the cloister's sides. The architecture was Greek: a large hall, and, at the end, the shrine with the god's statue. As the centuries passed, other buildings were added, and the second and greater of the two Alexandrian libraries—the "Daughter"—was arranged in them.

(v).   THE ROYAL TOMBS.

The "Soma" of Alexander became so famous that the earlier Ptolemies were buried close to it, and a mass of building—probably Greek in architecture—arose where the present Rue Rosette and Rue Nebi Daniel intersect. Later on, the burial place seems to have been in the Palace enclosure, and perhaps the "Mausoleum" where Cleopatra died was on the promontory of Silsileh, by a little Temple of Isis, within sound of the sea.

(vi).   OTHER BUILDINGS.

Theatre and Racecourse. Both were near the Palace: the former was probably on the site of the present Egyptian Government Hospital. Their architecture was Greek.

The Dyke of the Heptastadion was part of Alexander's scheme. But the Ptolemies completed it and fortified it where it rested on the Island of Pharos.

Such were the chief buildings and institutions that arose during the first hundred years of the city's life. Additions were made—notably the "Caesareum," begun by Cleopatra. But on the whole it may be said that Alexandria was the product of a single scheme, laid down by Dinocrates and executed by the first three

Ptolemies, and that she exhibited all the advantages, and perhaps some of the drawbacks, of a town that has been carefully planned. There was the majesty of well considered effects; but there also may have been a little dullness, and there were certainly none of the mysterious touches that reminded Athens and even Rome of an unanalysable past. In one sense the place was more Greek than Greece—built at a date when the Hellenic spirit had freed itself from many illusions and was winning a command over material forces that it had never possessed before. To her also Romance was added in time; but she started brand new, gleaming white, a calculated marvel of marble. Everything in her had been thought out—even her religion.

THE LATER PTOLEMIES (B.C. 221–51)
(*See Genealogical Tree p. 14*)

After the death of Euergetes, the dynasty declines. Some of his successors were able men, but a type evolved that made neither for morality nor for success. The average later Ptolemy is soft; he has the artistic temperament but no passionate love of art; he is born in the Palace at Alexandria and spends all his time there—so much so that it was not known for a year that Ptolemy IV had died; not naturally cruel, he is easily hurried into cruelty; he is unexpectedly shy; in his old age he grows fat, so that the Roman envoy murmurs "at all events the Alexandrians have seen their king walk" when Ptolemy VII comes puffing to greet him along the quay. And as the men soften, the women harden. The dynasty is interwoven with terrific queens. There is the Arsinoe whom Philadelphus married; there is Arsinoe III who faced the Syrian army at Rafa; there is Cleopatra III who murdered her son; and there is the last and greatest Cleopatra, with whom the tangled race expires.

In contrast to this confusion there rises the solid but unattractive figure of Rome (first embassy B.C. 273, first intervention B.C. 200). Her advance was postponed until she had gained the Western Mediterranean by defeating Carthage. She then came forward with studied politeness as the protector of liberty and morals in the East. Legal and self-righteous, she struck a chill into the whole Hellenistic world. She was horrified at its corruption—a corruption of which she never failed to take advantage, and the shattered empire of Alexander fell piece by piece into her hands. The Ptolemies were the allies of this impeccable creature—a curious alliance, but it lasted over 200 years. As the Egyptian fleet and army decayed, Rome's ministrations multiplied. She declared herself guardian of the dynasty; then that one of the Ptolemies had bequeathed Egypt to her in a will that she never produced. The dynasty became, with Ptolemy XIII, illegitimate, and Rome made him pay her to recognise his legitimacy. When he was driven from Egypt (B.C. 89) she made him pay her to restore him. He was escorted back by an army of creditors, and to raise the necessary sum of ten thousand talents he had to grind down the people with taxes. Rome was shocked, but firm.

Against this relentless advance Alexandria could do nothing. She was the brain of Egypt, and its five senses too and, as each embassy touched her quays, she realised, as the priest-ridden towns of the interior could not, that the glory was departing from the Nile. There was only one hope. Would Rome, before she could annex Egypt, fall to pieces herself? There were signs of it. The victorious republic had absorbed more plunder and more ideas than she could conveniently digest.

She had always found it particularly difficult to digest an idea. Rival Ptolemies had contended in Alexandria. But rival Romans were now contending in Rome. Might it be possible to play off against one the other, and so win through to safety? The scheme commended itself to the Alexandrians. It also occurred to the daughter of the bankrupt Ptolemy XIII, a beautiful and amusing princess called Cleopatra.

COINS OF LATER PTOLEMIES: Museum, Room 3.
PORTRAIT OF PTOLEMY IV: Museum, Room 12.
INSCRIPTION TO PTOLEMY VII: Museum, Garden Court.
CARICATURE OF ROMAN SENATOR as a rat: Museum, Room 13.

CLEOPATRA (B.C. 51–30)
(*See Genealogical Tree p. 14*)

The girl who came to the throne as Cleopatra VI Philopater was only seventeen. Her brother and husband Ptolemy XIV was ten; her younger brother eight, her sister fifteen. The Palace at Alexandria became a nursery, where four clever children watched the duel that was proceeding between Pompey and Caesar beyond the seas. Pompey was their guardian, but they had no illusions, either about him or one another. All they cared for was life and power. Cleopatra failed in her first intrigue, which was directed against her husband. He expelled her, and in her absence the duel was concluded. Pompey, defeated by Caesar, drifted to Egypt, threw himself on the mercy of his wards, and was murdered by their agents as he disembarked.

With the arrival of Caesar, Cleopatra's triumphs began. She did not differ in character from the other able and unscrupulous queens of her race, but she had one

source of power that they denied themselves—the
power of the courtesan—and she exploited it profes-
sionally. Though passionate, she was not the slave of
passion, still less of sentimentality. Her safety, and the
safety of Egypt were her care; the clumsy and amorous
Romans, who menaced both, were her natural prey. In
old times, a queen might rule from her throne. Now
she must descend and play the woman. Having heard
that Caesar was quartered at the Palace, Cleopatra returned to Alexandria, rolled herself up in a bale of
oriental carpets and was smuggled to him in this pi-
quant wrapper. The other children protested, but her
first victory had been won; she could count on the support of Julius Caesar against her husband.

Caesar's own position, was, however, most insecure.
He was Lord of the World, but in his haste to catch
Pompey he had hurried ahead of his legions. When the
glamour of his arrival had worn off the Alexandrians
realised this, and in a fierce little war (Aug. 48–Jan.
47) tried to crush him before reinforcements arrived.
He held the Palace (near Chatby); the Theatre (Egyptian Government Hospital); also part of the Eastern
Harbour where his small fleet lay. They held the rest
of the town, including the Western Harbour and the
Island, and they had with them Cleopatra's sister who
had escaped from the Palace and, later, Ptolemy XIV
himself,—so that they could claim to represent the
dynasty.

It was indeed a national rising against the Romans
and ably conducted. Five stages (*see* Map, p. 106).

(1). *Siege of the Palace.*—This was succeeding by land
but failed by sea, when Caesar, making a sudden excursion
down the docks of the Eastern Harbour, set fire to the
Alexandrian fleet. The flames spread to the Mouseion and
the Library ("Mother" Library) was burnt. An attempt to
contaminate the Palace water supply also failed; when the

Alexandrians pumped salt water into the conduit, the besieged Romans bored wells in the Palace enclosure.

(2). *First Naval Engagement.*—Caesar's reinforcements had begun to arrive, and a heavy east wind had carried them past the entrance of his harbour. He went out to tow them in, and the Alexandrians issued from their own harbour—the Western—to intercept him. They failed.

(3). *Second Naval Engagement and loss of the Island of Pharos.*—Issuing from his harbour, Caesar rounded Ras-el-Tin and deployed outside the line of reefs that stretch from it to Agame and guard the entrance to the Western Harbour. The Alexandrians waited inside. Dashing through the entrance he pressed them against the quays of Rhakotis and defeated them. Now he could attack the Island on both sides. On the following day it fell and he made it his headquarters, thus changing the strategy of the war.

(4). *Battle of the Dyke.*—Caesar now blocked up the arches that penetrated the Heptastadion so that the Alexandrians could not manœuvre from harbour to harbour. Then he tried to force his way into the town. He employed too many troops, and landing in his rear the Alexandrians threw him into confusion. He himself had to jump from the dyke and swim to a boat. Victory. They recaptured the whole of the Heptastadion and reopened its arches.

(5). *Battle by the Nile.*—The war was after all decided outside Alexandria. More reinforcements were coming to Caesar down the Canopic mouth of the Nile and the Alexandrians marched out to intercept them there. The young Ptolemy XIV was their general now. He was defeated and drowned, his army was destroyed, and Caesar returned in triumph to its city and to Cleopatra.

Cleopatra's fortune now seemed assured. Having married her younger brother (as Ptolemy XV) she went for a trip with Caesar up the Nile to show him its antiquities. The Egyptians detested her as their betrayer but she was indifferent. She bore Caesar a son and followed him to Rome, there to display her inso-

lence. She was at the height of her beauty and power
when the blow fell. On the Ides of March, B.C. 44,
Caesar was murdered. She had chosen the wrong lover
after all.

Back in Alexandria again, she watched the second
duel—that between Mark Antony and Caesar's murderers. She helped neither party, and when Antony
won he summoned her to explain her neutrality. She
came, not in a carpet but in a gilded barge, and her
life henceforward belongs less to history than to poetry.
It is almost impossible to think of the later Cleopatra
as an ordinary person. She has joined the company of
Helen and Iseult. Yet her character remained the
same. Voluptuous but watchful, she treated her new
lover as she had treated her old. She never bored him,
and since grossness means monotony she sharpened his
mind to those more delicate delights, where sense
verges into spirit. Her infinite variety lay in that. She
was the last of a secluded and subtle race, she was a
flower that Alexandria had taken three hundred years
to produce and that eternity cannot wither, and she
unfolded herself to a simple but intelligent Roman
soldier.

Alexandria, now reconciled to her fate and protected by the legions of Antony, became the capital of
the Eastern world. The Western belonged to Octavian,
Caesar's nephew, and a third duel was inevitable. It
was postponed for some years, during which Antony
acquired and deserted a Roman wife, and Cleopatra
bore him several children. Her son by Julius Caesar
was crowned as Ptolemy XVI, with the additional title
of King of Kings. Antony himself became a God, and
she built a temple to him, afterwards called the Caesareum, and adorned by two ancient obelisks (Cleopatra's Needles). This period of happiness and splendour ended in the naval disaster of Actium in the

Adriatic, where Octavian defeated their combined
fleets. The defeat was hastened by Cleopatra's coward-
ice. At the decisive moment she fled with sixty ships,
actually breaking her way through Antony's line from
the rear, and throwing it into confusion. He followed
her to Alexandria, and there, when the recriminations
had ceased, they resumed their life of pleasures that
were both shadowed and sharpened by the approach
of death. They made no attempt to oppose the pur-
suing Octavian. Instead, they formed a Suicide Club,
and Antony, to imitate the misanthrope Timon, built
a hermitage in the Western Harbour which he called
Timonium. Nor was religion silent. The god Hercules,
whom he loved and who loved him, was heard passing
away from Alexandria one night in exquisite music and
song.

Arrival of Octavian. He is one of the most odious of
the world's successful men and to his cold mind the
career of Cleopatra could appear as nothing but a vulgar debauch. Vice, in his opinion, should be furtive. At
his approach, Antony after resisting outside the Canopic Gate (at "Caesar's Camp") retreated into the city
and fell upon his sword. He was carried, dying, to Cleopatra, who had retired into their tomb, and their story
now rises to the immortality of art. Shakespeare drew
his inspiration from Plutarch, who was himself inspired, and it is difficult through their joint emotion to
realise the actual facts. The asp, for example, the asp
is not a certainty. It was never known how Cleopatra
died. She was captured and taken to Octavian, with
whom even in Antony's life-time she had been intri-
guing, for the courtesan in her persisted. She appeared
this time not in a carpet nor yet in a barge, but upon a
sofa, in the seductive negligence of grief. The good
young man was shocked. Realising that he intended
to lead her in his triumph at Rome, realising too that

she was now thirty-nine years old, she killed herself.
She was buried in the tomb with Antony; and her
ladies Charmion and Iras, who died with her, guarded
its doors as statues of bronze. Alexandria became the
capital of a Roman Province.

> COIN OF CLEOPATRA: Museum, Room 3.
> PORTRAIT OF CLEOPATRA (?): Museum, Room 12.
> DEATH OF CLEOPATRA in Plutarch, Shakespeare and
>   Dryden: Appendix p. 231.
> INSCRIPTION TO ANTONY: Museum, Room 6.
> COLOSSUS OF ANTONY: Museum, Garden Court.
> SITE OF CAESAREUM: p. 175.
> SHRINE OF POMPEY (?): p. 171.
> DEPARTURE OF THE GOD HERCULES: p. 104.

Thus the career of the Greco-Egyptian city closes,
as it began, in an atmosphere of Romance. Cleopatra
is of course a meaner figure than Alexander the Great.
Ambition with her is purely selfish; with Alexander it
was mystically connected with the welfare of mankind.
She knows nothing beyond the body and so shrinks
from discomfort and pain: Alexander attained the
strength of the hero. Yet for all their differences, the
man who created and the woman who lost Alexandria
have one element in common: monumental greatness;
and between them is suspended, like a rare and fragile
chain, the dynasty of the Ptolemies. It is a dynasty
much censored by historians, but the Egyptians, who
lived under it, were more tolerant. For it had one element of greatness: it did represent the complex country that it ruled. In Upper Egypt it carried on the tradition of the Pharaohs: on the coast it was Hellenistic
and in touch with Mediterranean culture. After its ex-
tinction, the vigour of Alexandria turns inwards. She
is to do big things in philosophy and religion. But she
is no longer the capital of a kingdom, no longer Royal.

PTOLEMAIC CULTURE

Before leaving the Ptolemies, let us glance back at
their civilisation. We have seen how they founded two
great institutions, the Palace and the Mouseion, which
communicated with one another, and which stretched
from the promontory of Silsileh to some point inland—
as far as the modern railway station, perhaps. It was
in this area, among gardens and colonnades, that the
culture of Alexandria came into being. The Palace provided the finances and called the tune: the Mouseion
responded with imagination or knowledge; the connection between them was so intimate as almost to be
absurd. When, for instance, Queen Berenice the wife
of Euergetes lost her hair from the temple where she
had dedicated it, it was the duty of the court astronomer to detect it as a constellation and of the court poet
to write an elegy thereon. And Stratonice, who was
perfectly bald, presented an even more delicate problem; she sent over a message to the Mouseion that
something must be written about her hair also. Victory
odes, Funeral dirges, Marriage hymns, jokes, genealogical trees, medical prescriptions, mechanical toys,
maps, engines of war: whatever the Palace required it
had only to inform the Mouseion, and the subsidised
staff set to work at once. The poets and scientists there
did nothing that would annoy the Royal Family and
not much that would puzzle it, for they knew that if
they failed to give satisfaction they would be expelled
from the enchanted area, and have to find another patron or starve. It was not an ideal arrangement, as out-
siders were prompt to point out, and snobbery and
servility taint the culture of Alexandria from the first.

It sprang up behind walls, it never knew loneliness, nor the glories and the dangers of independence, and the marvel is that it flourished as well as it did. At all events it is idle to criticise it for not being different, for if it had been different it would not have been Alexandrian. In spirit as in fact the Palace and the Mouseion touched, and the Palace was the stronger and the older. The contact strangled Philosophy and deprived Literature of such sustenance as Philosophy can bring to her. But it encouraged Science and gave even to Literature certain graces that she had hitherto ignored.

TEMPLE WHERE BERENICE DEDICATED HER HAIR: p. 196.

(A) LITERATURE

CALLIMACHUS, about 310–240.
APOLLONIUS OF RHODES, 260–188.
THEOCRITUS, about 320–250.

The literature that grew up in the Mouseion had no lofty aims. It was not interested in ultimate problems nor even in problems of behaviour, and it attempted none of the higher problems of art. To be graceful or pathetic or learned or amusing or indecent, and in any case loyal—this sufficed it, so that though full of experiments it is quite devoid of adventure. It developed when the heroic age of Greece was over, when liberty was lost and possibly honour too. It was disillusioned, and we may be glad that it was not embittered also. It had strength of a kind, for it saw that out of the wreck of traditional hopes three good things remained —namely the decorative surface of the universe, the delights of study, and the delights of love, and that of these three the best was love. Ancient Greece had also sung of love, but with restraint, regarding it as one activity among many. The Alexandrians seldom sang of anything else: their epigrams, their elegies and idylls, their one great epic, all turn on the tender passion, and celebrate it in ways that previous ages had never known, and that future ages were to know too well. Darts and hearts, sighs and eyes, breasts and chests, all originated in Alexandria and from the intercourse between Palace and Mouseion—stale devices to-day, but then they were fresh.

> *Who sculptured Love and set him by the pool,*
> *thinking with water such a fire to cool?**

runs a couplet ascribed to one of the early Librarians, and containing in brief the characteristics of the school —decorative method, mythological allusiveness, and the theme of love. Love as a cruel and wanton boy flits through the literature of Alexandria as through the thousands of terra cotta statuettes that have been exhumed from her soil; one tires of him, but it is appropriate that he should have been born under a dynasty that culminated in Cleopatra.

Literature took its tone from Callimachus—a fine poet, though not as fine as his patrons supposed. He began life as a schoolmaster at Eleusis (the modern Nouzha) and then was called to the Mouseion, where he became Librarian under Euergetes. His learning was immense, his wit considerable, his loyalty untiring. It was he who wrote the poem about Berenice's hair. Dainty and pedantic in all that he did, he announced that "a big book is a big nuisance" and cared more about neatness of expression than depth of feeling, though the feeling emerges in his famous epigram:

> *Someone told me, Heracleitus, of your end;*
> *and I wept, and thought how often you and I*

* Translated by R. A. Furness.

sunk the sun with talking. Well! and now you lie
antiquated ashes somewhere, Carian friend.
But your nightingales, your songs, are living still;
*them the death that clutches all things cannot kill.**

Only once was this exquisite career interrupted.
There was among his pupils a young man from Rhodes
with thin legs, by name Apollonius. Apollonius was
ambitious to write an Epic—a form of composition detested by Callimachus, and opposed to all his theories.
In vain he objected; Apollonius, then only eighteen,
gave in the Mouseion a public reading of the preliminary draft of his poem. A violent quarrel was the result,
Apollonius was expelled, and Callimachus wrote a sat-
ire called the Ibis, in which his rival's legs and other
deficiencies were exposed. The friends of Apollonius
retorted with equal spirit, and the tranquillity of the
Mouseion was impaired. Callimachus won, but his victory was not eternal; after his death Apollonius was
recalled to Alexandria, and in time became Librarian
there in his turn.

The Epic Apollonius insisted on writing has survived. It is modelled on Homer and deals with the voy-
age of the Argo to recover the Golden Fleece. But
there is nothing Homeric in the treatment and though
we are supposed to be in barbaric lands we never
really leave the cultivated court of the Ptolemies. Love
is still the ruling interest. He slips, the naughty little
boy, into the Palace of Medea, and shoots his tiny dart
at her, to inspire her with passion for Jason. So might
he have inspired Queen Berenice or Arsinoe. Pains,
languors, and raptures succeed, and the theme of the
heroic quest is forgotten. Callimachus can have found
nothing to object to in such a poem except its length,
for it is typical of his school. Its pictorial method is also
characteristic of Alexandria; many of the episodes

* Translated by R. A. Furness.

might be illustrated by terra cotta statues and gems.

But one of the poets who worked in the Mouseion—Theocritus—was a genius of a very different kind, a genius that Alexandria matured but cannot be said to have formed. Theocritus came here late in his career. He had been born at Cos and had lived in Sicily, and he arrived full of memories that no town-dweller could share—memories of fresh air and the sun, of upland meadows and overhanging trees, of goats and sheep, of the men and the women who looked after them, and of all the charm and the coarseness that go to make up country life. He had thrown these memories into poetical form, sometimes idealising them, sometimes giving them crudely, and he had called these poems Idylls—little pictures of rural existence. Love, mythological fancies, decorative treatment—he liked these things too, but he backed them with a width of experience and a zest for it that Callimachus and Apollonius never knew. While they are "Classics" who have to be studied, Theocritus appeals to us at once; his Fifteenth Idyll, describing life in the Greek Quarter at Alexandria, is as vivid now as when he wrote it. The dialogue with which it opens can be heard to-day in any of the little drawing rooms of Camp de César or Ibrahimieh. Praxinoe, a lady of the middle classes, is discovered seated, doing nothing in particular. In comes Gorgo, her friend.

Gorgo. Is Praxinoe at home?

Praxinoe. Oh my dear Gorgo, it's ages since you were here. She *is* at home. The wonder is that you've come even now. (calls to the maid). Eunoe, give her a chair and put a cushion on it.

Gorgo. Oh it does beautifully as it is.

Praxinoe. Sit down!

G. My nerves are all to bits—Praxinoe, I only just got here alive . . . . what with the crowd, what with the carriages . . . soldiers' boots—soldiers' great-coats, and the street's endless—you really live too far.

P. That's my insane husband. We took this hut—one can't call it a house—at the ends of the earth so that we shouldn't be neighbours. Mere jealousy. As usual.

G. But, dear, don't talk about your husband when the little boy's here—he's staring at you. (to the little boy) Sweet pet—that's all right—she isn't talking about papa.—Good Heavens, the child understands.—Pretty papa!

P. The other day, papa—we seem to call every day the other day—the other day he went to get some soda at the Baccal and brought back salt by mistake—the great overgrown lout.

G. Mine's exactly the same, he . . . . *

And so on. But Gorgo wants to go out again, in spite of her nerves. It is the Feast of the Resurrection—the Resurrection of Adonis—and there is to be a magnificent service inside the Palace, with a special singer. Praxinoe decides to venture too, and puts on the dress with the full body, that cost "at least eight pounds," excluding embroidery. They are ready at last and then the little boy begins to scream; he wishes to be of the party. But his mother remarks, "cry as much as you like, I cannot have you lamed," and takes Eunoe instead. In the street the crush is terrific, they are terrified of the Egyptians (just like Greek ladies to-day) and Eunoe, who is always awkward, nearly falls under a horse. The battle at the Palace Gate is worse still, Praxinoe's best muslin veil is torn, and she is more thankful than ever that she did not bring her little boy. But for a kind gentleman in the crowd, they would never have got in. Once inside, all is enjoyment. The draperies are gorgeous as might be expected when the Queen Arsinoe is paying for them—Arsinoe the wife of

---

* Adapted from Andrew Lang's Translation.

Philadelphus. And here is a Holy Sepulchre on which lies an image of Adonis, the down of early manhood just showing on his cheeks! The ladies are in ecstasies and can scarcely quiet themselves to listen to the Resurrection Hymn. In this Hymn Theocritus displays the other side of his genius—the "Alexandrian" side. He is no longer the amusing realist, but an erudite poet, whose chief theme is love.

O Queen that lovest Golgi and Idalium and Eryx, O Aphrodite that playest with gold—lo from the everlasting stream of Hades they have brought thee back Adonis. . . . . . A bridegroom of eighteen or nineteen years is he, his kisses are not yet rough, the golden down being yet on his lips. . . . . Thou only, dear Adonis, so men tell, visitest both this world and the stream of Hades. For Agamemnon had no such fate, nor Ajax the wrathful, nor Hector the first-born of Hecuba, nor Patroclus, nor Pyrrhus that returned out of Troy, nor the heroes of yet more ancient days. . . . . Be gracious now, dear Adonis, and bless us in the coming year. Dear has thy resurrection been, and dear shall it be when thou comest again.

A beautiful hymn; but as Gorgo remarks "all the same it's time to be getting home; my husband hasn't had his dinner and when he's kept waiting for his dinner he's as sour as vinegar." They salute the risen god, and go.

This delightful Idyll is not quite characteristic of Theocritus—he generally sings of Shepherds and their flocks. But it is his great contribution to the literature of Alexandria, and our chief authority for daily life under the Ptolemies. History is too much an affair of armies and kings. The Fifteenth Idyll corrects the error. Only through literature can the past be recovered and here Theocritus, wielding the double spell of realism and of poetry, has evoked an entire city from the dead

and filled its streets with men. As Praxinoe remarks of
the draperies "Why the figures seem to stand up and
to move, they're not patterns, they are alive."

The Mouseion was at its best under the first three
Ptolemies. Then it declined—at least in its literary output—and though Alexandria turned out poems, etc., for
several hundred years, few of them merit attention.
With the coming of the Romans her genius took a new
line, and essayed the neglected paths of philosophy
and religion. But she remained attractive to men of
letters, and nearly every writer of note visited her in
the course of his travels.

STATUETTES OF LOVES: Museum, Room 18.
NOUZHA (birthplace of Callimachus): p. 172.

(B) SCHOLARSHIP

In the Mouseion at Alexandria Greece first became
aware of her literary heritage, and the works of the
past were not only collected in the Library but were
codified, amended, and explained. Scholarship dates
from Zenodotus, the first Librarian. He turned his attention to Homer, divided the Iliad and Odyssey into
"Books," struck out spurious verses from the text,
marked doubtful ones, and introduced new readings.
He gave a general impulse to research. Hitherto the
Greek language had developed unnoticed. Now it was
consciously examined, and the result of the examina-
tion was the first Greek Grammar (about 100 B.C.).
Grammar is a valuable subject but also a dangerous
one, for it naturally attracts pedants and schoolmasters
and all who think that Literature is an affair of rules.
And the Grammarians of Alexandria forgot that they

were merely codifying the usages of the past, and presumed to dictate to the present, and to posterity; they set a bad example that has been followed for nearly 2,000 years. Greek accents—another doubtful boon—were also invented in the Mouseion. Indeed the whole of literary scholarship, as we know it, sprang up, including that curious by-product the Scholarly Joke. For instance: one learned man wrote a poem that had, when transcribed, the shape of a bird, another wrote a poem in the shape of a double-headed axe, and a third re-wrote the whole of the Odyssey without using the letter S. The donnish wit of the Mouseion infected the Palace, and was practiced by the Ptolemies themselves. One scholar, Sosibius by name, complained to King Philadelphus that he had not received his salary. The King replied, "The first syllable of your name occurs in Soter, the second in Sosigenes, the third in Bion, and the fourth in Apollonius; I have paid these four gentleman, and therefore I have paid you."

(C) ART

Unimportant. Alexandria had her special industries —*e.g.* glass, terra cotta, "Egyptian Queen" pottery, and woven stuffs, and her mint was famous; but for creative artists the Ptolemies looked over seas. Greek and Egyptian motives did not blend in Art as they did in Religion; attempts occur, but they are not notable and on the whole the city follows the general Hellenistic tendencies of the time. These tendencies led as we have seen away from the ideal and the abstract, and towards portraiture and the dainty and the picturesque. Men had lost for the time many illusions, both religious and political, and were trying to beautify their private lives, and the tombs of those whom they had loved.

GLASS AND "EGYPTIAN QUEEN" POTTERY: Museum, Room 17.

TERRA COTTAS: Museum, Room 18.

PTOLEMAIC COINS: Museum, Room 3.

BLEND OF GREEK AND EGYPTIAN MOTIVES: Museum, Rooms 11 and 15; also Kom es Chogafa Catacombs, (p. 163).

TOMB ORNAMENTS: Museum, Rooms 17–22.

(D) PHILOSOPHY

Unimportant. The Ptolemies imported some second-rate disciples of Aristotle to give tone to the Mouseion, but took no interest in the subject, and were indeed averse to it, since it might lead to freedom of thought. It was not until their dynasty was extinct that the great school of Alexandrian Philosophy arose. (See p. 64, under heading "The Spiritual City.")

(E) SCIENCE

The Ptolemies were more successful over Science than over Literature. They preferred it, for it could not criticise their divine right. Its endowment was the greatest achievement of the dynasty and makes Alexandria famous until the end of time. Science had been studied in Ancient Greece, but sporadically: there had been no co-ordination, no laboratories, and though important truths might be discovered or surmised, they were in danger of oblivion because they could not be popularised. The foundation of the Mouseion changed all this. Working under royal patronage and with every facility, science leapt to new heights, and gave valuable gifts to mankind. The third century B.C. is (from this point of view) the greatest period that civilisation has ever known—greater even than the nineteenth century A.D. It did not bring happiness or wisdom: science never does. But it explored the physical universe and harnessed many powers for our use. Mathematics, Geography, Astronomy, Medicine, all grew to maturity in the little space of the land between the present Rue Rosette and the sea, and if we had any sense of the fitting, some memorial to them would arise on the spot to-day.

(i). MATHEMATICS.

Mathematics begin with the tremendous but obscure career of Euclid. Nothing is known about Euclid: indeed one thinks of him to-day more as a branch of knowledge than as a man. But Euclid was once alive, landing here in the reign of Ptolemy Philadelphus, and informing that superficial monarch that there is "no royal road to geometry." Here he composed, among other works, his "Elements" in which he incorporated all previous knowledge, and which have remained the world's text book for Geometry almost down to the present day. Here he founded a mathematical school that lasted 700 years, and acknowledged his leadership to the last. Apollonius of Perga, who inaugurated the study of Conic Sections, was his immediate pupil: Hyspicles added to the thirteen books of his "Elements" two books more: and Theon—father to the martyred Hypatia—edited the "Elements" and gave them their present form, so that from first to last the mathematicians of Alexandria were preoccupied with him. An in-

THE WORLD ACCORDING TO ERATOSTHENES
B.C. 250

THE WORLD ACCORDING TO CLAUDIUS PTOLEMY
A.D. 100

significant man, according to tradition, and very shy; his snub to Philadelphus seems to have been exceptional.

(ii). GEOGRAPHY.

In Geography there are two leading figures—Eratosthenes and Claudius Ptolemy. Eratosthenes is the greater. He seems to have been an all round genius, eminent in literature as well as science. He was born at Cyrene in B.C. 276 and, on the death of Callimachus, was invited to Alexandria to become librarian. It was in the Mouseion observatory that he measured the Earth—perhaps not the greatest achievement of Alexandrian science, but certainly the most thrilling. His method was as follows. He knew that the earth is round, and he was told that the midsummer sun at Assouan in Upper Egypt cast no shadow at midday. At Alexandria, at the same moment, it did cast a shadow, Alexandria being further to the north on the same longitude. On measuring the Alexandria shadow he found that it was 7.⅕ degrees—*i.e.* ¹⁄₅₀th of a complete circle—so that the distance from Alexandria to Assouan must be ¹⁄₅₀th the circumference of the Earth. He estimated the distance at 500 miles, and consequently arrived at 250,000 miles for the complete circumference, and 7,850 for the diameter; in the latter calculation he is only 50 miles out. It is strange that when science had once gained such triumphs mankind should ever have slipped back again into fairy tales and barbarism.

The other great work of Eratosthenes was his "Geographies," including all previous knowledge on the subject, just as the "Elements" of Euclid had included all previous mathematical knowledge. The "Geographies" were in three books, and to them was attached a map of the known world. (See p. 42.) It is, of course, full of inaccuracies—*e.g.* Great Britain is too large, India fails to be a peninsula and the Caspian Sea connects with the Arctic Ocean. But it is conceived in the scientific spirit. It represents the world as Eratosthenes thought it was, not as he thought it ought to be. When he knows nothing, he inserts nothing; he is not ashamed to leave blank spaces. He bases it on such facts as he knew, and had he known more facts he would have altered it.

The other great geographer, Claudius Ptolemy, belongs to a later period (A.D. 100) but it is convenient to notice him here. Possibly he was a connection of the late royal family, but nothing is known of his life. His fame has outshone Eratosthenes', and no doubt he was more learned, for more facts were at his disposal. Yet we can trace in him the decline of the scientific spirit. Observe his Map of the World (p. 43). At first sight it is superior to the Eratosthenes Map. The Caspian Sea is corrected, new countries—*e.g.* China—are inserted, and there are (in the original) many more names. But there is one significant mistake. He has prolonged Africa into an imaginary continent and joined it up to China. It was a mere flight of his fancy: he even scattered this continent with towns and rivers. No one corrected the mistake and for hundreds of years it was believed that the Indian Ocean was land bound. The age of enquiry was over, and the age of authority had begun, and it is worth noting that the decline of science at Alexandria exactly coincides with the rise of Christianity.

(iii). ASTRONOMY AND THE CALENDAR.

Astronomy develops on the same lines as Geography. There is an early period of scientific research under Eratosthenes, and there is a later period in which Claudius Ptolemy codifies the results and dictates his opinions to posterity. He announced, for example, that the Universe revolves round the Earth, and this "Ptolemaic" Theory was adopted by all subsequent astronomers until Galileo, and supported by all the thunders of the Church. Yet another view had been put forward, though Ptolemy ignores it. Aristarchus of Samos, working at Alexandria with Eratosthenes, had suggested that the earth might revolve round the sun, and it is only a chance that this view was not stamped as official and imposed as orthodox all through the Middle Ages. We do not know what Aristarchus' arguments were, for his writings have perished, but we may be sure that, working in the 3rd century B.C., he had arguments and did not take refuge in authority. Astronomy under the Ptolemies was a serious affair—lightened only by the episode of Berenice's Hair.

As to the Calendar. The Calendar we now use was worked out in Alexandria. The Ancient Egyptians had calculated the year at 365 days. It is actually 365¼, so before long they were hopelessly out; the official Harvest Festival, for instance, only coincided with the actual harvest once in 1,500 years. They were aware of the discrepancy, but were too conservative to alter it: that was left to Alexandria. In B.C. 239 the little daughter of Ptolemy Euergetes died, and the priests of Serapis at Canopus passed a decree making her a goddess. A reformer even in his grief, the King induced them to rectify the Calendar at the same time by decreeing the existence of a Leap Year, to occur every four years, as at present; he attempted to harmonise the traditions of Egypt with the science of Greece. The attempt—so typical of Alexandria—failed, for though the priests passed the decree they kept to their old chronology. It was not until Julius Caesar came to Egypt that the cause of reform prevailed. He established the "Alexandrian Year" as official, and modelled on it the "Julian," which we use in Europe to-day; the two years were of the same length, but the "Alexandrian" retained the old Egyptian arrangement of twelve equal months.

(iv). MEDICINE.

Erasistratus (3rd. cent. B.C.) is the chief glory of the Alexandrian medical school. In his earlier life he had been a great practitioner, and had realised the connection between sexual troubles and nervous breakdowns. In his old age he settled in the Mouseion, and devoted himself to research. He practised vivisection on animals, and possibly on criminals, and he seems to have come near to discovering the circulation of the blood. Less severely scientific were the healing cults that sprang up in the great temples of Serapis, both at Alexandria and at Canopus;—cults that were continued into Christian times under other auspices.

SITE OF MOUSEION: p. 113.
MAP OF ERATOSTHENES: p. 42.
MAP OF CLAUDIUS PTOLEMY: p. 43.
TEMPLE OF SERAPIS AT CANOPUS: p. 190.
  „   „   ALEXANDRIA: p. 157.

SECTION II

Christian Period

THE RULE OF ROME (B.C. 30–A.D. 313)

Octavian (Augustus) the founder of the Roman Empire, so disliked Alexandria that after his triumph over Cleopatra he founded a town near modern Ramleh—Nicopolis, the "City of Victory." He also forbade any Roman of the governing classes to enter Egypt without his permission, on the ground that the religious orgies there would corrupt their morals. The true reason was economic. He wanted to keep the Egyptian corn supply in his own hands, and thus control the hungry populace of Rome. Egypt, unlike the other Roman provinces, became a private appanage of the Emperor, who himself appointed the Prefect who governed it, and Alexandria turned into a vast imperial granary where the tribute, collected in kind from the cultivators, was stored for transhipment. It was an age of exploitation. Octavian posed locally as the divine successor of the Ptolemies, and appears among hieroglyphs at Dendyra and Philae. But he had no local interest at heart.

After his death things improved. The harsh ungenerous Republic that he had typified passed into Imperial Rome, who, despite her moments of madness, brought happiness to the Mediterranean world for two hundred years. Alexandria had her share of this happiness. Her new problem—riots between Greeks and Jews—was solved at the expense of the latter; she gained fresh trade by the improved connections with India (Trajan A.D. 115, recut the Red Sea Canal); she was visited by a series of appreciative Emperors on their way to the antiquities of Upper Egypt.

In about A.D. 250 she, with the rest of the Empire, re-entered trouble. The human race, as if not designed to enjoy happiness, had slipped into a mood of envy and discontent. Barbarians attacked the frontiers of the Empire, while within were revolts and mutinies. The difficulties of the Emperors were complicated by a religious problem. They had, for political reasons, been emphasising their own divinity—a divinity that Egypt herself had taught them: it seemed to them that it would be a binding force against savagery and schism. They therefore directed that everyone should worship them. Who could have expected a protest, and a protest from Alexandria?

RAMLEH (Nicopolis): p. 181.
STATUE OF EMPEROR (Marcus Aurelius): Museum, Room 12.
IMPERIAL COINS: Museum, Room 2.
CERTIFICATES TO ROMAN SOLDIERS: Museum, Room 6.

THE CHRISTIAN COMMUNITY

According to the tradition of the Egyptian Church, Christianity was introduced into Alexandria by St. Mark, who in A.D. 45 converted a Jewish shoemaker named Annianus, and who in 62 was martyred for protesting against the worship of Serapis. There is no means of checking this tradition; the origins of the movement were unfashionable and obscure, and the authorities took little notice of it until it disobeyed their

regulations. Its doctrines were confounded partly with
the Judaism from which they had sprung, partly with
the other creeds of the city. A letter ascribed to the
Emperor Hadrian (in Alexandria, 134) says, "Those
who worship Serapis are Christians, and those who call
themselves bishops of Christ are devoted to Serapis,"
showing how indistinct was the impression that the
successors of St. Mark had made. The letter continues,
"As a race of men they are seditious, vain, and spiteful;
as a body, wealthy and prosperous, of whom nobody
lives in idleness. Some blow glass, some make paper,
and others linen. Their one God is nothing peculiar;
Christians, Jews, and all nations worship him. I wish
this body of men was better behaved."

The community was organised under its "overseer"
or bishop, who soon took the title of patriarch, and appointed bishops elsewhere in Egypt. The earliest centres were (i) the oratory of St. Mark which stood by
the sea shore—probably to the east of Silsileh—and was
afterwards enlarged into a Cathedral; (ii) a later cathedral church dedicated (285) by the Patriarch Theonas to the Virgin Mary; it was on the site of the
present Franciscan Church by the Docks; (iii) a Theological College—the "Catechetical School," founded
about 200, where Clement of Alexandria and Origen
taught—site unknown.

It was its "bad behaviour," to use Hadrian's term,
that brought the community into notice—that is to say,
its refusal to worship the Emperors. To the absurd
spiritual claims of the state, Christianity opposed the
claims of the individual conscience, and the conflict
was only allayed by the state itself becoming Christian.
The conflict came to its height in Alexandria, which,
more than any other city in the Empire, may claim to
have won the battle for the new religion. Persecution,
at first desultory, grew under Decius, and culminated

in the desperate measures of Diocletian (303)—demolition of churches, all Christian officials degraded, all Christian non-officials enslaved. Diocletian, an able ruler—the great column miscalled Pompey's is his memorial—did not persecute from personal spite, but the results were no less appalling and definitely discredited the pagan state. While we need not accept the Egyptian Church's estimate of 144,000 martyrs in nine years, there is no doubt that numbers perished in all ranks of society. Among the victims was St. Menas, a young Egyptian soldier who became patron of the desert west of Lake Mariout, where a great church was built over his grave. St. Catherine of Alexandria is also said to have died under Diocletian, but it is improbable that she ever lived; she and her wheel were creations of Western Catholicism, and the land of her supposed sufferings has only recognised her out of politeness to the French. The persecution was vain, the state was defeated, and the Egyptian Church, justly triumphant, dates its chronology, not from the birth of Christ, but from the "Era of Martyrs" (A.D. 284). A few years later the Emperor Constantine made Christianity official, and the menace from without came to an end.

COIN OF HADRIAN AT ALEXANDRIA: Museum, Room 2.
SITE OF ST. MARK'S: p. 178.
CAPITAL FROM ST. MARK'S: Museum, Room 1.
SITE OF ST. THEONAS: p. 184.
COLUMN FROM ST. THEONAS: p. 177.
STATUE OF DIOCLETIAN: Museum, Room 17.
COINS OF DIOCLETIAN: Museum, Room 4.
"POMPEY'S (Diocletian's) Pillar": p. 157.
CHURCH OF ST. MENAS: p. 210.
REMAINS FROM ST. MENAS: Museum, Rooms 1, 2, 5.
MODERN CHURCH OF ST. CATHERINE: p. 155.
PILLAR OF ST. CATHERINE: p. 114.

CERTIFICATE OF HAVING WORSHIPPED THE GODS: Museum, Room 6.

ARIUS AND ATHANASIUS (4th Cent. A.D.)

It was natural that Alexandria, who had suffered so much for Christianity, should share in its triumph, and as soon as universal toleration was proclaimed her star re-emerged. Rome, as the stronghold of Paganism, was discredited, and it seemed that the city by the Nile might again become Imperial, as in the days of Antony. That hoped was dashed, for Constantine, a very cautious man, thought it safer to found a new capital on the Bosphorus, where no memories from the past could intrude. But Alexandria was the capital spiritually, and at least it seemed that she, who had helped to free imprisoned Christendom, would lead it in harmony and peace to its home at the feet of God. That hope was dashed too. An age of hatred and misery was approaching. The Christians, as soon as they had captured the machinery of the pagan state, turned it against one another, and the century resounds to a dispute between two dictatorial clergymen.

Both were natives of Alexandria. Arius, the older, took duty at St. Mark's—the vanished church by the sea at Chatby where the Evangelist was said to have been martyred. Learned and sincere, tall, simple in his dress, persuasive in his speech, he was accused by his enemies of looking like a snake, and of seducing, in the theological sense, 700 virgins. Athanasius, his opponent, first appears as a merry little boy, playing with other children on the beach below St. Theonas—on the shore of the present western harbour, that is to say. He was playing at Baptism, which not being in orders he had no right to do, and the Patriarch, who happened to be looking out of the palace window, tried to stop him. No one ever succeeded in stopping St. Athanasius. He baptised his playmates, and the Patriarch, struck by his precocity, recognised the sacrament as valid and engaged the active young theologian as his secretary. Physically Athanasius was blackish and small, but strong and extremely graceful—one recognises a modern street type. His character can scarcely be discerned through the dust of the century, but he was certainly not loveable, though he lived to be a popular hero. His powers were remarkable. As a theologian he knew what is true, and as a politician he knew how truth can be enforced, and his career blends subtlety with vigour and self-abnegation with craft in the most remarkable way.

The dispute—Arius started it—concerned the nature of Christ. Its doctrinal import is discussed below (p. 80); here we are only dealing with the outward results. Constantine who was no theologian and dubiously Christian, was appalled by the schism which rapidly divided his empire. He wrote, counselling charity, and when he was ignored summoned the disputants to Nicaea on the Black Sea (325). Two hundred and fifty bishops and many priests attended, and amid great violence the *Nicene Creed* was passed, and Arius condemned. Athanasius who was still only a deacon, returned in triumph to Alexandria, and soon afterwards became Patriarch here. But his troubles were only beginning. Constantine, still obsessed with hopes of toleration, asked him to receive Arius back. He refused, and was banished himself.

He was banished five times in all—once by the orthodox Constantine (335), twice by the Arian Constantius (338 and 356), once by the pagan Julian (362), and once, shortly before his death, by the Arian Valens.

Sometimes he hid in the Libyan desert, sometimes he escaped to Rome or Palestine and made Christendom ring with his grievances. Twice he came near to death in church—once in the Caesareum where he marched processionally out of one door as the enemy came in at the other, and once in St. Theonas at night, where he escaped from the altar just before the Arian soldiers attacked him there. He always returned, and he had the supreme joy of outliving Arius, who fell down dead one evening, while walking through Alexandria with a friend. To us, living in a secular age, such triumphs appear remote, and it seems better to die young, like Alexander the Great, than to drag out this arid theological Odyssey. But Athanasius has the immortality that he would have desired. Owing to his efforts the Church has accepted as final his opinion on the nature of Christ, and, duly grateful, has recognised him as a doctor and canonised him as a saint. In Alexandria a large church was built to commemorate his name. It stood on the north side of the Canopic Street; the Attarine Mosque occupies part of its site to-day.

St. Mark's: p. 178.
St. Theonas': p. 184.
Council of Nicaea, picture of: p. 114.
Nicene Creed: original text containing Clause against
    Arius: Appendix p. 236.
Caesareum: p. 175.
Attarine Mosque (Church of St. Athanasius): p. 155.

THE RULE OF THE MONKS
(4th and 5th Cents.)

Theophilus.
Cyril.
Dioscurus.

After the exploits of Athanasius the Patriarchate of Alexandria became very powerful. In theory Egypt belonged to the Emperor, who sent a Prefect and a garrison from Constantinople; in practise it was ruled by the Patriarch and his army of monks. The monks had not been important so long as each lived alone, but by the 4th cent. they had gathered into formidable communities, whence they would occasionally make raids on civilisation like the Bedouins to-day. One of these communities was only nine miles from Alexandria (the "Ennaton"), others lay further west, in the Mariout desert; of those in the Wady Natrun, remnants still survive. The monks had some knowledge of theology and of decorative craft, but they were averse to culture and incapable of thought. Their heroes were St. Ammon who deserted his wife on their wedding eve, or St. Antony, who thought bathing sinful and was consequently carried across the canals of the delta by an angel. From the ranks of such men the Patriarchs were recruited.

Christianity, which had been made official at the beginning of the 4th century, was made compulsory towards its close, and this gave the monks the opportunity of attacking the worship of Serapis. Much had now taken refuge in that ancient Ptolemaic shrine— philosophy, magic, learning, licentiousness. The Patriarch Theophilus led the attack. The Serapis temple at Canopus (Aboukir) fell in 389, the parent temple at Alexandria two years later; great was the fall of the latter, for it involved the destruction of the Library whose books had been stored in the cloisters surrounding the buildings; a monastery was installed on the site. The persecution of the pagans continued, and culminated in the murder of Hypatia (415). The achievements of Hypatia, like her youthfulness, have been exaggerated; she was a middle-aged lady who taught mathematics at the Mouseion and though she was a philosopher too we have no record of her doctrines. The monks were now supreme, and one of them had murdered the Imperial Prefect, and had been canonised for the deed by the Patriarch Cyril. Cyril's wild black army filled the streets, "human only in their faces," and anxious to perform some crowning piety before they retired to their monasteries. In this mood they encountered Hypatia who was driving from a lecture (probably along the course of the present Rue Nebi Daniel), dragged her from the carriage to the Caesareum, and there tore her to pieces with tiles. She is not a great figure. But with her the Greece that is a spirit expired—the Greece that tried to discover truth and create beauty and that had created Alexandria.

The monks however, have another aspect. They were the nucleus of a national movement. Nationality did not exist in the modern sense—it was a religious not a patriotic age. But under the cloak of religion racial passions could shelter, and the monks killed Hypatia not only because they knew she was sinful but also because they thought she was foreign. They were anti-Greek, and later on they and their lay adherents were given the name of Copts. "Copt" means "Egyptian." The language of the Copts was derived from the ancient Egyptian, their script was Greek, with the addition of six letters adapted from the hieroglyphs. The new movement permeated the whole country, even cosmopolitan Alexandria, and as soon as it found a theological formula in which to express itself, a revolt against Constantinople broke out.

That formula is known as "Monophysism." Its theological import—it concerns the Nature of Christ—is discussed below (p. 81); here we are concerned with its outward effects. The Patriarch Dioscurus, successor and nephew to Cyril, is the first Monophysite hero and the real founder of the Coptic Church. The Emperor took up a high and mighty line, and at the Council of Chalcedon near Constantinople Dioscurus was exiled and his doctrines condemned (451). From that moment no Greek was safe in Egypt. The racial trouble, which had been averted by the Ptolemies, broke out at last and has not even died down to-day. Before long Alexandria was saddled with two Patriarchs. There was (i) The Orthodox or "Royal" Patriarch, who upheld the decrees of Chalcedon. He was appointed by the Emperor and had most of the Church revenues. But he had no spiritual authority over the Egyptians; to them he was an odious Greek official, disguised as a priest. (ii) The Monophysite or Coptic Patriarch, who opposed Chalcedon—a regular Egyptian monk, poor, bigoted and popular. Each of these Patriarchs claimed to represent St. Mark and the only true church; each of them is represented by a Patriarch in Alexandria to-day. Now and then an Emperor tried to heal the schism, and made concessions to the Egyptian faith. But the schism was racial, the concessions theological, so nothing was effected. Egypt was only held for the Empire by Greek garrisons, and consequently when the Arabs came they conquered her at once.

TOMBSTONES FROM THE ENNATON: Museum, Room 1.
WADY NATRUN: p. 216.
TEMPLE OF SERAPIS AT CANOPUS: p. 190.
TEMPLE OF SERAPIS AT ALEXANDRIA: p. 157.
CAESAREUM: p. 175.
ORTHODOX AND COPTIC PATRIARCHATES: pp. 227, 228.
PORTRAIT OF DIOSCURUS: p. 223.

THE ARAB CONQUEST (641)

We are now approaching the catastrophe. Its details though dramatic are confusing. It took place during the reign of the Emperor Heraclius, and we must begin by glancing at his curious career.

Heraclius was an able and sensitive man—very sensitive, very much in the grip of his own moods. Sometimes he appears as a hero, a great administrator; sometimes as an apathetic recluse. He won his empire (610) by the sword; then the reaction came and he allowed the Persians to occupy Syria and Egypt almost without striking a blow. Alexandria fell by treachery. She was safe on the seaward side, for the Persians had no fleet, and her immense walls made her impregnable by land; their army (which was encamped near Mex) could burn monasteries but do nothing more. But a foreign student—Peter was his name—got into touch with them and revealed the secrets of her topography. A canal ran through her from the Western Harbour, rather to the north of the present (Mahmoudieh) canal, and it passed, by a bridge, under the Canopic Way (present Rue Sidi Metwalli). The harbour end of the canal was unguarded, and a few Persians, at Peter's advice, disguised themselves as fishermen and rowed in; then walked westward down the Canopic Way and unbarred the Gate of the Moon to the main army (617). Their rule was not cruel; though sun-worshippers, they persecuted neither orthodox Christians nor Copts. For five years Heraclius did nothing; then shook off his torpor and performed miracles. Marching against the armies of the Persians in Asia, he defeated them and recovered the relic of the True Cross, which

they had taken from Jerusalem. Alexandria and Egypt
were freed, and at the festival of the Exaltation of the
Cross—his coins comemmorate it—the Emperor appeared as the champion of Christendom and the greatest ruler in the world. It is unlikely that in the hour of
his triumph he paid any attention to the envoys of an
obscure Arab Sheikh named Mohammed, who came
to congratulate him on his victory and to suggest that
he should adopt a new religion called "Peace" or
"Islam." But he is said to have dismissed them politely.
The same Sheikh also sent envoys to the Imperial Viceroy at Alexandria. He too was polite and sent back a
present that included an ass, a mule, a bag of money,
some butter and honey, and two Coptic maidens. One
of the latter, Mary, became the Sheikh's favourite con-
cubine. Amidst such amenities did our intercourse with
Mohammedanism begin.

Heraclius, now at the height of his power and with
a mind now vigorous, turned next to the religious problem. He desired that his empire should be spiritually
as it was physically one, and in particular that the feud
in Egypt should cease. He was not a bigot. He believed
in tolerance, and sought a formula that should satisfy
both orthodox and Copts—both the supporters and the
opponents of the Council of Chalcedon. A disastrous
search. He had better have let well alone. The formula
that he found—Monothelism—was so obscure that no
one could understand it, and the man whom he chose
as its exponent was a cynical bully, who did not even
wish that it should be understood. This man was Cyrus,
sometimes called the Mukaukas, the evil genius of
Egypt and of Alexandria. Cyrus was made both Patriarch and Imperial Viceroy. He landed in 631, made no
attempt to conciliate or even to explain, persecuted the
Copts, tried to kill the Coptic Patriarch and at the end
of ten years' rule had ripened Egypt for its fall. There

was a Greek garrison in Alexandria and another to the
south of the present Cairo in a fort called "Babylon."
And there were some other forces in the Delta and the
fleet held the sea. But the mass of the people were
hostile. Heraclius ruled by violence, though he did not
realise it; the reports that Cyrus sent him never told
the truth. Indeed, he paid little attention to them; he
was paralysed by a new terror: Mohammedanism. His
nerve failed him again, as at the Persian invasion. Syria
and the Holy Places were again lost to the Empire, this
time for ever. Broken in health and spirits, the Emperor slunk back to Constantinople, and there, shortly
before he died, Cyrus arrived with the news that Egypt
had been lost too.

What happened was this. The Arab general Amr
had invaded Egypt with an army of 4,000 horse. Amr
was not only a great general. He was an administrator,
a delightful companion, and a poet—one of the ablest
and most charming men that Islam ever produced. He
would have been remarkable in any age; he is all the
more remarkable in an age that was petrified by theology. Riding into Egypt by the coast where Port Said
stands now, he struck swiftly up the Nile, defeated an
Imperial army at Heliopolis and invested the fort of
Babylon. Cyrus was inside it. His character, like the
Emperor's, had collapsed. He knew that no native
Egyptian would resist the Arabs, and he may have felt,
like many of his contemporaries, that Christianity was
doomed, that its complexities were destined to perish
before the simplicity of Islam. He negotiated a peace,
which the Emperor was to ratify. Heraclius was furious
and recalled him to Constantinople. But the mischief
had been done; all Egypt, with the exception of Alexandria, had been abandoned to the heathen.

Alexandria was surely safe. In the first place the
Arabs had no ships, and Amr, for all his courage, was

not the man to build one. "If a ship lies still," he writes, "it rends the heart; if it moves it terrifies the imagination. Upon it a man's power ever diminishes and calamity increases. Those within it are like worms in a log, and if it rolls over they are drowned." Alexandria had nothing to fear on the seaward side from such a foe and on the landward what could he do against her superb walls, defended by all the appliances of military science? Amr, though powerful, had no artillery. His was purely a cavalry force. And there was no great alarm when, from the southeast, the force was seen approaching and encamping somewhere beyond the present Nouzha Gardens. Moreover the Patriarch Cyrus was back, and had held a great service in the Caesareum and exhorted the Christians to arms. Indeed it is not easy to see why Alexandria did fall. There was no physical reason for it. One is almost driven to say that she fell because she had no soul. Cyrus, for the second time, betrayed his trust. He negotiated again with the Arabs, as at Babylon, and signed (Nov. 8th, 641) an armistice with them, during which the Imperial garrison evacuated the town. Amr did not make hard terms; cruelty was neither congenial to him nor politic. Those inhabitants who wished to leave might do so; the rest might worship as they wished on payment of tribute.

The following year Amr entered in triumph through the Gate of the Sun that closed the eastern end of the Canopic Way. Little had been ruined so far. Colonnades of marble stretched before him, the Tomb of Alexander rose to his left, the Pharos to his right. His sensitive and generous soul may have been moved, but the message he sent to the Caliph in Arabia is sufficiently prosaic. "I have taken," he writes, "a city of which I can only say that it contains 4,000 palaces, 4,000 baths, 400 theatres, 1,200 greengrocers and 40,-

ooo Jews." And the Caliph received the news with
equal calm, merely rewarding the messenger with a
meal of bread and oil and a few dates. There was nothing studied in this indifference. The Arabs could not
realise the value of their prize. They knew that Allah
had given them a large and strong city. They could
not know that there was no other like it in the world,
that the science of Greece had planned it, that it had
been the intellectual birthplace of Christianity. Leg-
ends of a dim Alexander, a dimmer Cleopatra, might
move in their minds, but they had not the historical
sense, they could never realise what had happened on
this spot nor how inevitably the city of the double harbour should have arisen between the lake and the sea.
And so though they had no intention of destroying her,
they destroyed her, as a child might a watch. She
never functioned again for over 1,000 years.

One or two details are necessary, to complete this
sketch of the conquest. It had been a humane affair,
and no damage had been done to property; the Library
which the Arabs are usually accused of destroying had
already been destroyed by the Christians. A few years
later, however, some damage was done. Supported by
an Imperial fleet, the city revolted, and Amr was
obliged to re-enter it by force. There was a massacre,
which he stayed by sheathing his sword; the Mosque
of Amr or of Mercy was built upon the site. As gover-
nor of Egypt, he administered it well, but his interests
lay inland not on the odious sea shore, and he founded
a city close to the fort of Babylon—Fostat, the germ of
the modern Cairo. Here all the life of the future was to
centre. Here Amr himself was to die. As he lay on his
couch a friend said to him: "You have often remarked
that you would like to find an intelligent man at the
point of death, and to ask him what his feelings were.
Now I ask *you* that question." Amr replied, "I feel as if

the heaven lay close upon the earth and I between the two, breathing through the eye of a needle." There is something in this dialogue that transports us into a new world; it could never have taken place between two Alexandrians.

COIN OF HERACLIUS, SHOWING CROSS: Museum, Room 4.
ROSETTA GATE (Gate of the Sun): p. 132.
MOSQUE OF AMR: p. 157.

Such were the chief physical events in the city during the Christian Period. We must now turn back to consider another and more important aspect: the spiritual.

SECTION III

The Spiritual City

INTRODUCTION

When Cleopatra died and Egypt became part of the Roman Empire, it seemed that the career of Alexandria was over. Her life had centred round the Ptolemies who had adorned her with architecture and scholarship and song, and when they were withdrawn what remained? She was just a provincial capital. But the vitality of a city is not thus measured. There is a splendour that kings do not give and cannot take away, and just when she lost her outward independence she was recompensed by discovering the kingdom that lies within. Three sections of her citizens—Jews, Greeks and Christians—were attracted by the same spiritual problem, and tried to solve it in the same way.

The Problem. It never occurred to these Alexandrian thinkers, as it had to some of their predecessors in ancient Greece, that God might not exist. They assumed that he existed. What troubled them was his relation to the rest of the universe and particularly to man. Was God close to man? Or was he far away? If close, how could he be infinite and eternal and omnipotent? And if far away, how could he take any interest in man, why indeed should he have troubled to create him? They wanted God to be both far and close.

The Solution. Savages solve such a problem by

having two gods—a pocket fetich whom they beat when he irritates them, and a remote spirit in the sky, and they do not try to think out any connection between the two. The Alexandrians, being cultivated, could not accept such crudities. Instead, they assumed that between God and man there is an intermediate being or beings, who draw the universe together, and ensure that though God is far he shall also be close. They gave various names to this intermediate being, and ascribed to him varying degrees of dignity and power. But they became as certain of his existence as of God's, for in philosophy their temperament was mystic rather than scientific, and as soon as they hit on an explanation of the universe that was comforting, they did not stop to consider whether it might be true.

After this preliminary, let us approach the three great sections of Alexandrian thought.

I. THE JEWS

THE SEPTUAGINT—about B.C. 200.
THE WISDOM OF SOLOMON—about B.C. 100.
PHILO—cont. with Christ.

The seat of the Jews was Jerusalem, where they had evolved their cult of Jehovah and built him his unique temple. But as soon as Alexandria was founded they began to emigrate to the lucrative and seductive city, and to take up their quarters near the modern Ibrahimieh. Soon a generation arose that was Greek in speech. The Hebrew Scriptures had to be translated for their benefit, and seventy rabbis—so the legend goes—were shut up by Ptolemy Philadelphus in seventy huts on the island of Pharos, whence they simul-

taneously emerged with seventy identical translations
of the Bible. This was the famous Septuagint version
—made as a matter of fact over many years, and not
completed till B.C. 130.

But the new generation was Greek in spirit as well
as speech, and diverged increasingly from the conservative Jews at Jerusalem. Both sections worshipped
Jehovah, but the Alexandrian grew more and more
conscious of the churlishness and inaccessibility of his
national god. Thought mingled with his adoration.
How could he link Jehovah to man? And, utilising a
few hints in the orthodox scriptures, he produced as
his first attempt a fine piece of literature called "The
Wisdom of Solomon"; it is at present included in the
Apocrypha. The author—his name is unknown—not
only wrote in Greek but had studied Stoic and Epicu-
rean Philosophy and Egyptian rites. He had the cosmopolitan culture of Alexandria. And, solving his problem
in the Alexandrian way, he conceived an intermediate
between Jehovah and man whom he calls Sophia or
Wisdom.

> Wisdom is more moving than any motion: she goeth
> through all things by reason of her pureness. Being but
> one she can do all things and in all ages entering into
> holy souls she makes them friends of God, and prophets.
> She is more beautiful than the sun and all the order of
> stars: being compared with the light she is found beyond
> it. For after this cometh night, but vice shall not prevail
> against wisdom.

In such a passage Wisdom is more than "being wise."
She is a messenger who bridges the gulf and makes us
friends of God.

In Philo the Jewish school of Alexandria reaches its
height. Little is known of his life. His brother was head

of the Jewish community here and he himself was sent (A.D. 40) on a disastrous embassy to the mad Emperor Caligula at Rome.

Being an orthodox Jew, he states his philosophic problem in the language of the Old Testament. Thus:—

Jehovah had said I AM THAT I AM—that is to say, nothing can be predicated about God except existence. God has no qualities, no desires, no form, and no home. We cannot even call God "God" because "God" is a word, and no word can describe God. While to regard him as a man is to commit "an error greater than the sea." GOD IS, and no more can be said of him.

Yet this unapproachable being has created us. How? And why?

Through his Logos or Word. This Logos of Philo is, like "Wisdom," a messenger who bridges the gulf. He is the outward expression of God's existence. He created and he sustains the world, and Philo uses the actual language of devotion concerning him, calling him Israel the Seer, the Dove, the Dweller in the Inmost, —language which naturally recalls and possibly suggested the opening of St. John's Gospel. "In the beginning was the Word, and the Word was with God." Philo might have written this. But he could not have written "the Word was God" nor "the Word was made flesh" for it was, as we shall see, the distinction of Christianity to conceive that the link between man and God should be himself both God and man.

By this doctrine of the Logos, Philo made the Hebrew Jehovah intelligible and acceptable to the Alexandrian Jews. It is a doctrine not found in the Old Testament, and to extract it he had to employ allegory and to wrest words from their natural meanings. This gives his philosophy a frigid timid air, and obscures its real sublimity. Only once or twice does he break loose, and declare that the path to truth lies not through allegory but through vision. "Those who can see" he exclaims, "lift their eyes to heavens, and contemplate the Manna, the divine Logos. Those who cannot see, look at the onions in the ground." After his death, the Jews of Alexandria accomplished no more in philosophy. They had stated the problem. The restatement was for the Greeks and the Christians.

JEWISH INSCRIPTIONS FROM IBRAHIMIEH: Museum, Room 21.

II. NEO-PLATONISM

PLOTINUS (204–262).
PORPHYRY (233–306).
HYPATIA (d. 415).

The Ptolemies had imported some Greek philosophers, as part of the personnel of the Mouseion, but they were second-rate, and it was not until the Ptolemies had passed away, and the city herself was declining, that philosophy took root and bore the white mystic rose of Neo-Platonism. It developed out of a doctrine of Plato's. Six hundred years before, Plato had taught at Athens that the world we live in is an imperfect copy of an ideal world. He had also taught other things, but this was the doctrine that the "New Platonists" of Alexandria took up and pursued to sublime and mystic conclusions. Whatever Plato had thought of this world as a philosopher, he had enjoyed it as a citizen and a poet, and has left delightful accounts of it in his dialogues. The Neo-Platonists were more logical. Since this world is imperfect, they regarded it as negligible, and excluded from their writings all references to daily life. They might be disembodied spirits, freed from locality and time, and it is only after careful study that we realise that they too were human,—nay, that they were typically Alexandrian, and that in them the later city finds her highest expression.

The School was founded by Ammonius Saccas, who had begun life as a porter in the docks, and as a Christian, but abandoned both professions for the study of Plato. Nothing is known of his teaching, but he produced great pupils—Longinus, Origen, and, greatest of all, Plotinus. Plotinus was probably born at Assiout; probably; no one could find out for certain because he was reticent about it, saying that the descent of his soul into his body had been a great misfortune, which he did not desire to discuss. He completed his main training at Alexandria, and then took part in a military expedition against Persia, in order to get into touch with Persian thought (Zoroastrianism), and with Indian thought (Hinduism, Buddhism). He must have made a queer soldier and he was certainly an unsuccessful one, for the expedition suffered defeat, and Plotinus was very nearly relieved of the disgrace of having a body. Escaping, he made his way to Rome, and remained there until the end of his life, lecturing. In spite of his sincerity, he became fashionable, and the psychic powers that he had acquired not only gained him, on four occasions, the Mystic Vision which was the goal of his philosophy, but also discovered a necklace which had been stolen from a rich lady by one of her slaves. He was indifferent to literary composition; after his death his pupil Porphyry collected his lecture-notes and published them in nine volumes—the "Enneads." The Enneads are ill arranged and often obscure. But they contain a logical system of thought, some account of which must be attempted—Alexandria produced nothing greater. And they deal with the usual Alexandrian problem—the linking up of God and man.

Like Philo, and like the Christians, Plotinus believes in God, and since his God has three grades, we may almost say that he believes in a Trinity. But it is very different to the Christian Trinity, and even more difficult to understand. The first and highest grade in it he calls the One. The One is—Unity, the One. Nothing else can be predicated about it, not even that it exists; it is more incomprehensible than the Jehovah of Philo; it has no qualities, no creative force, it is good only as the goal of our aspirations. But though it cannot create, it overflows (somewhat like a fountain), and from its overflow or emanation is generated the second grade of the Trinity—the "Intellectual Principle." The Intellectual Principle is a little easier to understand than the "One" because it has a remote connection with our lives. It is the Universal mind that contains—not all things, but all thoughts of things, and by thinking it creates. It thinks of the third grade—the All Soul—which accordingly comes into being. With the All Soul we near the realm of the comprehensible. It is the cause of the Universe that we know. All that we grasp through the senses was created by it—the Gods of Greece, etc., in the first place, then the demi-gods and demons, then, descending in the scale, ourselves, then animals, plants, stones; matter, that seems so important to us, is really the last and feeblest emanation of the All Soul, the point at which creative power comes to a halt.—And these three grades, the "One," the "Intellectual Principle," and the "All Soul," make up between them a single being, GOD; who is three in one and one in three, and the goal of all creation.

Thus far the system of Plotinus may appear unattractive as well as abstruse; we must now look at the other and more emotional side. Not only do all things flow from God; they also strive to return to him; in other words, the whole Universe has an inclination towards good. We are all parts of God, even the stones, though we cannot realise it; and man's goal is to become actually, as he is potentially, divine. Therefore rebirth is permitted, in order that we may realise God better in a future existence than we can in this; and therefore the Mystic Vision is permitted, in order that, even in this existence we may have a glimpse of God. God is ourself, our true self, and in one of the few literary passages in the Enneads, the style of Plotinus catches fire from his thought and we are taught in words of immortal eloquence, how the Vision may be obtained.

But what must we do? How lies the path? How come to vision of the inaccessible Beauty, dwelling as if in consecrated precincts, apart from the common ways where all men may see?

"Let us flee to the beloved Fatherland." This is the soundest counsel. But what is the flight? How are we to gain the open sea?

The Fatherland is There whence we have come, and There is the Father.

What then is our course, what the manner of our flight? This is not a journey for the feet; the feet bring us only from land to land; all this order of things you must set aside and refuse to see; you must close the eyes and call instead upon another vision which is to be waked within you, a vision the birth-right of all, which few can see. . . . .

Withdraw into yourself and look. And if you do not find yourself beautiful yet, act as does the creator of a statue that is to be made beautiful; he cuts away here, he smooths there, he makes this line lighter, that purer, until a lovely face has grown upon his work.

When you know that you have become this perfect

work, when you are self-gathered in the purity of your being, nothing now remaining that can shatter that inner unity—when you perceive that you have grown to this, you are now become very vision; now call up all your confidence, strike forward yet a step—you need a guide no longer—forward yet a step—you need a guide no longer —strain and see.

This is the only eye that sees the mighty Beauty. If the eye that ventures the vision be dimmed by vice, impure or weak, then it sees nothing even though another point to what lies plain before it. To any vision must be brought an eye adapted to what is to be seen, and having some resemblance to it. Never did eye see the sun unless it had first become sunlike, and never can the soul have vision of the first Beauty unless itself be beautiful.*

This sublime passage suggests three comments, with which our glance at Plotinus must close. In the first place its tone is religious, and in this it is typical of all Alexandrian philosophy. In the second place it lays stress on behaviour and training; the Supreme Vision cannot be acquired by magic tricks—only those will see it who are fit to see. And in the third place the vision of oneself and the vision of God are really the same, because each individual *is* God, if only he knew it. And here is the great difference between Plotinus and Christianity. The Christian promise is that a man shall see God, the Neo-Platonic—like the Indian—that he shall be God. Perhaps, on the quays of Alexandria, Plotinus talked with Hindu merchants who came to the town. At all events his system can be paralleled in the religious writings of India. He comes nearer than any other Greek philosopher to the thought of the East.

Porphyry, the pious disciple of Plotinus, was himself a philosopher of note, and the Neo-Platonic School

* S. McKenna's Translation.

continued to flourish all through the 4th cent. Its main temper kept the same; it was pessimistic as regards the actual world and actual men, but optimistic as regards the future because it believed that the world and all in it has emanated from God and has been granted the means of reverting to him. It recognised the presence of Evil but not its eternal existence, and consequently it was a practical support to its believers, and upheld the last of them, Hypatia, through martyrdom.

> *When I do contemplate your words and you*
> *revered Hypatia, then I kneel to view*
> *the Virgin's starry home; there in the skies*
> *your works and perfect words I recognise,*
> *a star unsullied of instruction wise.**

Thus wrote an unknown admirer at the beginning of the 5th century. None of Hypatia's discourses have been preserved, but we know that with her and with her father, Theon, the great tradition of Plotinus expired at Alexandria.

III. CHRISTIANITY

INTRODUCTION

Percolating through the Jewish Communities, the Christian religion reached Egypt as early as the 1st cent. A.D. On its arrival, it found, already established there, two distinct forms of spiritual life.

The first was the spiritual life of Ancient Egypt, which had clung to the soil of the Nile valley for over 4,000 years. It had existed so long that though Chris-

---

* Translated by R. A. Furness.

tianity could close its temples she never quite up-
rooted it from the heart of the people. The resurrection
of Osiris as Sun God; the partaking of him as Corn God
by the blessed in the world below; the beneficent
group of the mother Isis with Horus her child; the same
Horus as a young warrior slaying the snaky Set; the
key-shaped "ankh" that the gods and goddesses carried
as a sign of their immortality:—these symbols had sunk
too deeply into the minds of the native Egyptians to
be removed by episcopal decrees. Consequently there
were cases of reversion—e.g. at Menouthis (near Aboukir) in 480, when some villagers were discovered
worshipping the ancient deities in a private house. And
there were also cases of confusion, where the old religion passed imperceptibly into the new. Did Christianity borrow from the Osiris cult her doctrines of the
Resurrection and Personal Immortality, and her sacrament of the Eucharist? The suggestion has been made.
It is more certain that she borrowed much of her sym-
bolism and popular art. Isis and Horus become the
Virgin and Child, Horus and Set St. George and the
Dragon, while the "ankh" appears unaltered on some
of the Christian tombstones as a looped cross, and
slightly altered on others as a cross with a handle.

The second form of spiritual life was the life of Alexandria. Its quality (mainly Hellenic and philosophic)
has already been indicated. Christianity, to begin with
was not philosophic, being addressed to poor and
unfashionable people in Palestine. But as soon as it
reached Alexandria its character altered, the turning
point in its worldly career arrived. The Alexandrians
were highly cultivated, they had libraries where all the
wisdom of the Mediterranean was accessible, and their
faith inevitably took a philosophic form. Occupied by
their favourite problem of the relation between God
and man, they at once asked the same question of the

new religion as they asked the Jews and the Greeks—namely, What is the link? Philo said the Logos, Plotinus the Emanations. The new religion replied "Christ." There was nothing startling to the Alexandrians in such a reply. Christ too was the Word, he too proceeded from the Father. His incarnation, his redemption of mankind through suffering—even these were not strange ideas to people who were accustomed to "divine" kings, and familiar with the myths of Prometheus and Adonis. Alexandrian orthodoxy, Alexandrian heresies, both centred round the problem that was familiar to Alexandrian paganism—the relation between God and man.

Thus Christianity did not burst upon Egypt or upon Alexandria like a clap of thunder, but stole into ears already prepared. Neither on her popular nor on her philosophic side was she a creed apart. Only politically did she stand out as an innovator, through her denial of divinity to the Imperial Government at Rome.

ANKH: Museum, Room 8.
EARLY CHRISTIAN CROSSES: Museum, Room 1.
ISIS AND HORUS: Museum, Room 10.
MENOUTHIS: p. 197.

(1). GNOSTICISM (Esoteric knowledge)

CERINTHUS—About 100 A.D.
BASILIDES—120.
VALENTINUS—140.

Gnosticism taught that the world and mankind are the result of an unfortunate blunder. God neither created us nor wished us to be created. We are the work of an inferior deity, the Demiurge, who wrongly believes himself God, and we are doomed to decay. But God, though not responsible for our existence, took pity on it, and has sent his Christ to counteract the ignorance of the Demiurge and to give us Gnosis (knowledge). Christ is the link between the divine and that unfortunate mistake the human.

The individual Gnostics played round this idea. Cerinthus (educated here) taught that Jesus was a man, and Christ a spirit who left him at death. Basilides (a Syrian visitor) that there were three dispensations, pre-Jewish, Jewish, and Christian, each of whose rulers had a son, which son comprehended more of God than did his father. The Ophites worshipped snakes because the serpent in Eden was really a messenger from God, who induced Eve to disobey the Demiurge Jehovah. Consequently if we wish to be good we must be bad —a conclusion that was also reached, though by a different route, by Carpocrates, who organised an Abode of Love on one of the Greek islands. These are unsavoury charlatans. But one of the Gnostics—Valentinus —was a man of another stamp, and his system has a tragic quality most rare in Alexandria.

Valentinus (probably an Egyptian; educated here; taught mainly at Rome) held the usual Gnostic doctrine that creation is a mistake. But he tried to explain how the mistake came about. He imagines a primal God, the centre of a divine harmony, who sent out manifestations of himself in pairs of male and female. Each pair was inferior to its predecessor, and Sophia ("wisdom") the female of the thirtieth pair, least perfect of all. She showed her imperfection not, like Lucifer, by rebelling from God, but by desiring too ardently to be united to him. She fell through love. Hurled from the divine harmony, she fell into matter, and the universe is formed out of her agony and remorse. She herself was rescued by the first Christ but not before she had borne a son, the Demiurge, who rules this world of sadness and confusion, and is incapable of realising anything beyond it. In this world there are three classes of men, all outwardly the same, men of the Body, the Spirit, and the Soul. The first two belong to the Demiurge and ought to obey him. The third are really the elect of his mother Sophia. He rules them but cannot make them obey. It was for their salvation that the Christ whom we call Jesus descended straight from the primal God and left with his twelve disciples the secret tradition of the Gnosis.

With Valentinus the Gnosticism of Alexandria reaches its height. Further east it took other forms. It had spread by 150 A.D. all round the Mediterranean, and threatened to defeat orthodox Christianity. But it was pessimistic, imaginative, esoteric—three great obstacles to success. It was not a creed any society could adopt, being anti-social, and by the time of Constantine its vogue was over.

GNOSTIC AMULETS: Museum, Room 17.

(II). ORTHODOXY (Early)

CLEMENT OF ALEXANDRIA—about 200.
ORIGEN—185–253.

Orthodoxy at Alexandria did not begin on clear-cut lines; indeed the more we look at it the more it melts into its surroundings. It adapted from Philo his doctrine of the Logos, and identified the Logos with Christ. It shared with Gnosticism the desire for knowledge of God, while declaring that such knowledge need not be esoteric. It has its special Gospel—St. Mark's—but other Gospels, since condemned as uncanonical, were equally read in its churches, e.g. the Gospels of the

Hebrews and of the Egyptians. It was permeated by Greek thought—Neo-Platonists became Christians, and vice versa. But one distinguishing doctrine it did have —the supreme value of Christ. Christ was the "Word" incarnate, through whom the love and power of God could alone be "known." Problems as to Christ's nature did not trouble the earlier theologians. Their impulse was to testify, not to analyse. A feeling of joy inspires their interminable writings, and it is possible to detect through their circumlocution the faith that steeled the martyrs, their contemporaries.

Clement of Alexandria (probably a Greek from Athens) was head of the big Theological College here. His problem, like that of the Jews before him, was to recommend his religion to a subtle and philosophic city, and his methods forestall those of the advanced missionary to-day. He does not denounce Greek philosophy. His line is that it is a preparation for the Gospel, that the Jewish law was also a preparation, and that all that happened before the birth of Christ is indeed a divine approach to that supreme event. Learned and enlightened, he set Christianity upon a path that she did not long consent to follow. He raised her from intellectual obscurity, he lent her for a little Hellenic persuasion, and the graciousness of Greece seems in his pages not incompatible with the Grace of God.

> He is the greatest in the Kingdom of Heaven who shall do and teach in imitation of God by showing free Grace like His; for the bounties of God are for the common benefits.

Only in Alexandria could such a theologian have arisen.

His work was carried on by his pupil Origen, the strangest and most adventurous of the Early Fathers. Gentle and scholarly by nature, Origen had an instinct for self-immolation that troubled his life and the lives of his friends. He was an Egyptian (the name is connected with Horus), and he was born here of Christian parents and tried as a boy to share his father's martyrdom at the Temple of Serapis. Calmed for a while, he supported his mother and brothers, and was fellow pupil with Plotinus. Then he became head of the Theological College, and having attained fame as a teacher and lay preacher, castrated himself (a "Eunuch for the Kingdom of Heaven's sake."—Matt. xix, 12). His patron, the Bishop of Alexandria, disowned him for this, and ruled that he could not now take orders; other bishops declared that he could, and the Christian communities were divided by the grotesque controversy. Origen was considerate and even repentant; he had no wish to cause scandal, and when ordered to leave Alexandria he obeyed. But his opinions ever verged towards the incorrect; he believed, like Plotinus, in pre-existence, he disbelieved in the eternity of punishment, and it is with the greatest hesitation that orthodoxy has received him to her bosom. In the main he developed the theory of his master Clement—that Christianity is the heir of the past and the interpreter of the future, —and he taught that Christ has been with mankind not only at his incarnation but since the beginning of creation, and has in all ages linked them, according to their capacity, with God.

Thus the characteristic of early orthodoxy was a belief in Christ as the link between God and man. A humanising belief; the work of the Greek scholars who had subtilised and universalised the simpler faith of Palestine, and had imparted into it doctrines taught by Paganism. We must now watch it harden and transform. Several causes transformed it—e.g. the growth of an ignorant monasticism in Egypt, the growth in

Northern Africa, of a gloomier type of Christianity under Tertullian, and the general spirit of aggression the new religion everywhere displayed as soon as Constantine labelled it as official. But there was one cause that was inherent in the belief itself, and that alone concerns us here. Christ was the Son of God. All agreed. But what was the *Nature* of Christ? The subtle Alexandrian intellect asked this question about the year 300, and the Arian heresy was the result. It asked it again about 400 and produced the Monophysite heresy. And a third query about 600 produced a third heresy, the Monothelite. Let us glance at these three in turn. Heresies to others, they were of course orthodox in their own eyes. Each believed itself the only interpreter of the link that binds God to man.

UNCANONICAL GOSPELS: Appendix p. 235.

(III). ARIANISM

Christ is the Son of God. Then is he not younger than God? Arius held that he was and that there was a period before time began when the First Person of the Trinity existed and the Second did not. A typical Alexandrian theologian, occupied with the favourite problem of linking human and divine, Arius thought to solve the problem by making the link predominately human. He did not deny the Godhead of Christ, but he did make him inferior to the Father—of *like* substance, not of the *same* substance, which was the view held by Athanasius, and stamped as orthodox by the Council of Nicaea. Moreover the Arian Christ, like the Gnostic Demiurge, made the world;—creation, an inferior activity, being entrusted to him by the Father, who had Himself created nothing but Christ.

It is easy to see why Arianism became popular. By

making Christ younger and lower than God it brought
him nearer to us—indeed it tended to level him into a
mere good man and to forestall Unitarianism. It appealed to the untheologically minded, to emperors
and even more to empresses. But St. Athanasius, who
viewed the innovation with an expert eye, saw that
while it popularised Christ it isolated God, and he
fought it with vigour and venom. His success has been
described (p. 52). It was condemned as heretical in
325, and by the end of the century had been expelled
from orthodox Christendom. Of the theatre of this ancient strife no trace remains at Alexandria; the church
of St. Mark where Arius was presbyter has vanished:
so have the churches where Athanasius thundered—St.
Theonas and the Caesareum. Nor do we know in
which street Arius died of epilepsy. But the strife still
continues in the hearts of men, who always tend to
magnify the human in the divine, and it is probable
that many an individual Christian to-day is an Arian
without knowing it.

NICENE CREED (original text): Appendix p. 236.
PICTURE OF COUNCIL OF NICAEA: p. 114.

(IV).   MONOPHYSISM ("Single Nature")

Christ is the Son of God, but also the Son of Mary.
Then has he two natures or one? The Monophysites
said "One." They did not deny Christ's incarnation, but
they asserted that the divine in him had quite absorbed the human. The question was first raised in cler-
ical circles in Constantinople, but Alexandria took it up
hotly, and "Single Nature" became the national cry of
Egypt. We have already seen (p. 56) the political importance of this heresy, how it was connected with a
racial movement against the Greeks, how when it was

condemned at Chalcedon (451) Egypt slipped into permanent mutiny against the Empire. The Council announced that Christ had two natures, unmixed and unchangeable but at the same time indistinguishable and inseparable. This is the orthodox view—the one we hold. The Copts (and Abyssinians) are still Monophysites, and consequently not in communion with the rest of Christendom.

COPTIC CHURCH: pp. 175, 229.

(v).   MONOTHELISM ("Single Will")

As the minds of the Alexandrians decayed, their heresies became more and more technical. Arianism enshrines a real problem which the layman as well as the cleric can apprehend. Monophysism is more remote. And Monothelism is difficult to state in the language of theology, and almost impossible to state in the language of common sense. Perhaps it bears in it the signs of carelessness, for as we have seen (p. 59) it was the invention of the Emperor Heraclius in the last desperate days when he was trying to conciliate Egypt.

If Christ has one Nature he has of course one will. But suppose he has two Natures. How many wills has he then? The Monothelites said "One." The orthodox view—the one we hold—is "Two, one human the other divine, but both operating in unison." Obscure indeed is the problem, and we can well believe that the Alexandrians, against whom the Arabs were then marching, did not understand Monothelism when it was hurriedly explained to them by a preoccupied general. But it was not without a future. It failed as a compromise but survived as a heresy, and long after the Imperial Government had disowned it and Egypt had fallen to

Islam, it was cherished in the uplands of Syria by the Maronite Church.

MARONITE CHURCH: pp. 153, 229.

CONCLUSION: ISLAM

We have now seen Alexandria handle one after another the systems that entered her walls. The ancient religion of the Hebrews, the philosophy of Plato, the new faith out of Galilee—taking each in turn she has left her impress upon it, and extracted some answer to her question, "How can the human be linked to the divine?"

It may be argued that this question must be asked by all who have the religious sense, and that there is nothing specifically Alexandrian about it. But no; it need not be asked; it was never asked by Islam, by the faith that swept the city physically and spiritually into the sea. "There is no God but God, and Mohammed is the Prophet of God," says Islam, proclaiming the needlessness of a mediator; the man Mohammed has been chosen to tell us what God is like and what he wishes, and there all machinery ends, leaving us to face our Creator. We face him as a God of power, who may temper his justice with mercy, but who does not stoop to the weakness of Love, and we are well content that, being powerful, he shall be far away. That old dilemma, that God ought at the same time to be far away and close at hand, cannot occur to an orthodox Mohammedan. It occurs to those who require God to be loving as well as powerful, to Christianity and to its kindred growths, and it is the weakness and the strength of Alexandria to have solved it by the conception of a link. Her weakness: because she had always to be shifting the link up and down—if she got it too near God it was too far from man, and *vice versa*. Her strength: because she did cling to the idea of Love, and much philosophic absurdity, much theological aridity, must be pardoned to those who maintain that the best thing on earth is likely to be the best in heaven.

Islam, strong through its abjuration of Love, was the one system that the city could not handle. It gave no opening to her manipulations. Her logoi, her emanations and aeons, her various Christs, orthodox, Arian, Monophysite, or Monothelite—it threw them all down as unnecessary lumber that do but distract the true believer from his God. The physical decay that crept on her in the 7th century had its counterpart in a spiritual decay. Amr and his Arabs were not fanatics or barbarians and they were about to start near Cairo a new Egypt of their own. But they instinctively shrank from Alexandria; she seemed to them idolatrous and foolish; and a thousand years of silence succeeded them.

INSCRIPTION FROM KORAN (Terbana Mosque): p. 136.

SECTION IV

Arab Period

THE ARAB TOWN (7th–16th Cents.)

During the thousand years and more that intervene between the Arab conquest of Egypt and its conquest by Napoleon, the events in the history of Alexandria are geographic rather than political. Neglected by man, the land and the waters altered their positions, and could Alexander the Great have returned he would have failed to recognise the coast. (i) The fundamental change was in the 12th cent., when the Canopic mouth of the Nile silted up. Consequently the fresh water lake of Mariout, being no longer fed by the Nile floods, also silted and ceased to be navigable. Alexandria was cut off from the entire river system of Egypt, and could not flourish until it was restored; she has always required the double nourishment of fresh water and salt. (ii) There was also a change in the outline of the city: the dyke Heptastadion, built by the Ptolemies to connect the mainland with the island of Pharos, fell into ruin and became a backbone along which a broad spit of land accreted; and so Pharos turned from an island into a peninsula—the present Ras-el-Tin.

The Arabs, though they let the city fall out of repair, admired it greatly. One of them writes as follows:—

The city was all white and bright by night as well as by day. By reason of the walls and pavements of white marble the people used to wear black garments; it was

the glare of the marble that made the monks wear black.
So too it was painful to go out by night . . . . . . a tailor
could see to thread his needle without a lamp. No one
entered without a covering over his eyes.

A second writer describes the green silk awnings that
were spread over the Canopic Way. A third, even
more enthusiastic exclaims:—

I have made the Pilgrimage to Mecca sixty times, but
if Allah had suffered me to stay a month at Alexandria
and pray on its shores, that month would be dearer to
me.

The Arabs were anything but barbarians; their own
great city of Cairo is a sufficient answer to that charge.
But their civilisation was Oriental and of the land; it
was out of touch with the Mediterranean civilisation
that has evolved Alexandria. At first they made some
effort to adapt it to their needs. The church of St. Theonas became part of the huge "Mosque of the 1,000
Columns"; the church of St. Athanasius also became a
Mosque—the present Attarine Mosque occupies part of
its site; and a third Mosque, that of the Prophet Daniel,
rose on the Mausoleum of Alexander. But the Caesareum, the Mouseion, the Pharos, the Ptolemaic Palace,
all became ruinous. So did the walls. And though the
Arabs built new walls in 811, their course is so short
that they vividly illustrate the decline of the town and
of the population. (See map p. 106). They only enclosed a fragment of the ancient city.

In 828 the Venetians, according to their own account, stole from Alexandria the body of St. Mark, con-
cealing it first in a tub of pickled pork in order to repel
the attentions of the Moslem officials on the quay. The
theft was a pardonable one, for the Arabs never seemed
to know that it had been made; it occasioned much
satisfaction in Venice and no inconvenience in Alex-

andria. St. Mark procured, there was little to attract
the European world; the ports of Egypt were now Rosetta (Bolbitine Mouth of the Nile), and Damietta
(Phatnitic Mouth); there was no reason to approach
Alexandria now that her water system had collapsed.
Towards the end of the Arab rule she did indeed re-
gain some slight importance; the Mameluke Sultan of
Cairo, Kait Bey, built on the ruins of the Pharos the
fine fort that bears his name (1480). He built it as a
defence against the growing naval power of the Turks.
The Turks conquered Egypt in 1517, and a new but
equally unimportant chapter in the history of Alexandria begins.

St. Theonas: p. 184.
Attarine Mosque: p. 155.
Mosque of the Prophet Daniel: p. 112.
Fragment of Arab Wall: pp. 113, 170.
Fort Kait Bey: p. 144.

THE TURKISH TOWN (16th–18th Cents.)

Under the Turks the population continued to shrink,
so that eventually the narrow enclosure of the Arab
walls became too large. A new settlement sprang up
on the neck of land that had formed between the two
harbours. It still exists and is known as the "Turkish
Town." A second-rate affair; little more than a strip of
houses intermixed with small mosques; a meagre copy
of Rosetta, where the architecture of these centuries
can best be studied. So unimportant a place can have
no connected history. All that one can do is to quote
the isolated comments of a few travellers. (i) The
English sailor, John Foxe, (1577) has a lively tale to

tell. He had been caught by the Turkish corsairs and imprisoned with his mates. With the connivance of a friendly Spaniard he organised a mutiny, recaptured his ship and in true British style worked it out of the Eastern Harbour under the fire of the guns on Kait Bey. (ii) John Sandys (1610) gives a quaint but impressive description of the decay:—

> Such was this Queen of Cities and Metropolis of Africa: who now hath nothing left her but ruins; and those ill witnesses of his perished beauties: declaring rather that towns as well as men have the ages and destinies . . . . . Sundry Mountains were raised of the ruins, by Christians not to be mounted; lest they should take too exact a survey of the city: in which are often found, (especially after a shower) rich stones and medals engraven with the figure of their Gods and men with such perfection of Art as these now cut seeme lame to those and unlively counterfeits.

(iii) Captain Norden, a Dane, (1757) was in an irritable mood, as the Turks would not let him sketch the fortifications. The English community was already in existence, and the Captain's account of it makes interesting if painful reading:—

> They keep themselves quiet and conduct themselves without making much noise. If any nice affair is to be undertaken they withdraw themselves from it and leave to the French the honour of removing all difficulties. When any benefits result from it they have their share and if affairs turn out ill they secure themselves in the best manner they can.

(iv) Another irritable visitor landed here in 1779— the lively but spiteful Mrs. Eliza Fay. Being a Christian, she was not allowed to disembark in the Western Harbour nor to ride any animal nobler than a donkey. She visited Cleopatra's Needles and "Pompey's Pillar,"

VRAY PORTRAICT DE LA VILLE D'ALE- Lac d'eau doulce de moult grande estendu
XANDRIE EN EGYPTE & grand revenue en poisson

TERRE FERME D'AFRIQUE

LAC MAREOTIS

MOSAYEE

COLONNE DE PONPEE

ENTREE DV NIL

PORTA DEL PEPE

CHATEAV NEVF

CHATEAV VIEL

PORTO VECHIO

PORTE DE LA MARINE

OBELISQUE

PALAIS DE ALEXANDRE

PHARVS

CASTELETO

GARDPHALO

PORTE DV CAIRE

FORES DE PALMIERS

LA MER MEDITERRANEE

Calque par E. Zaccar.
Calque par R. Palacios

Extrait des *Observations de plusieurs singularitez etc.*
par Pierre Belon du Mans
Paris 1554

then writes to her sister, "I certainly deem myself very fortunate in quitting this place so soon." She makes no mention of the English community, but was entertained by the Prussian Consul, and has left an unflattering account of his stout wife.

There are some old maps, compiled from the accounts of travellers, but bearing little reference to reality. That of Pierre Belon (1554) is reproduced on p. 89. Its main errors are the introduction of the Nile, and the outflow of Lake Mariout to the sea. It shows the two harbours, the Arab walls, Cleopatra's Needles, "Pompey's Pillar" and the Canopic or Rosetta Gate (Porte du Caire). The Turkish town has not yet been built. De Monconys' map of 1665—*see* frontispiece—is in some ways still more absurd; Cleopatra's Needle has turned into a pyramid. The mound in the right centre is meant for Fort Cafarelli. The beginnings of the Turkish Town appear on Ras-el-Tin. In 1743 Richard Pocock published the first scientific map in his "Description of the East"; measurements and soundings are given. Captain Norden the Dane brought out a good pictorial plan of the "New," *i.e.* Eastern Harbour, showing the seamarks. And the exact extent of Alexandria's decay is shown in the magnificent map published by the French expedition under Napoleon. There we see that the Arab enclosure is empty except for a few houses on Kom-el-Dik and by the Rosetta Gate, and that the population—only 4,000—is huddled into the wall-less Turkish Town.

With Napoleon a new age begins.

TURKISH TOWN: p. 134.
ROSETTA: p. 199.
CLEOPATRA'S NEEDLES: p. 175.
"POMPEY'S PILLAR": p. 157.
FORT CAFARELLI: p. 183.

SECTION V

Modern Period

NAPOLEON (1798–1801)

On July 1st 1798 the inhabitants of the obscure town saw that the deserted sea was covered with an immense fleet. Three hundred sailing ships came out from the west to anchor off Marabout Island, men disembarked all night and by the middle of next day 5,000 French soldiers under Napoleon had occupied the place. They were part of a larger force, and had come under the pretence of helping Turkey, against whom Egypt was then having one of her feeble and periodic revolts. The future Emperor was still a mere general of the French Republic, but already an influence on politics, and this expedition was his own plan. He was in love with the East just then. The romance of the Nile valley had touched his imagination, and he knew that it was the road to an even greater romance—India. At war with England, he saw himself gaining at England's expense an Oriental realm and reviving the power of Alexander the Great. In him, as in Mark Antony, Alexandria nourished imperial dreams. The expedition failed but its memory remained with him: he had touched the East, the nursery of kings.

Leaving Alexandria at once, he marched on Cairo and won the battle of the Pyramids. Then an irreparable disaster befell him. He had left his admiral, Brueys, with instructions to dispose the fleet as safely as possible, since Nelson was known to be in pursuit. Under

modern conditions Brueys would have sailed into the
Western Harbour, but in 1798 the reefs that cross the
entrance had not been blasted away, and though the
transports got in the passages were rather dangerous
for the big men of war. Brueys was nervous and
thought he had better take them round to an anchorage, supposed impeccable, in the Bay of Aboukir. Nelson followed him, attacked him unexpectedly and destroyed his fleet. Details of this famous engagement,
the so-called "Battle of the Nile," are given in another
place (p. 191); its result was to lose for Napoleon the
command of the sea. The French expedition took Cairo
and remained powerful on land, but could receive no
reinforcements, no messages, and withered away like
a plant that has been cut at the root. Turkey declared
against it, and a Turkish force, supported by British
ships, landed at Aboukir (July 1799). Here Napoleon
was successful. He commanded in person and in a series of brilliant engagements drove the invaders into
the sea: this is the "Land" battle of Aboukir (described
in detail p. 192). But his dreams had been shattered
by Nelson. He saw that his destiny, whatever it was,
would not be accomplished in the East, and meanly
deserting his army he slipped back to France.

We now come to the first British expedition, and to
its successful and interesting campaign. In March 1801
Sir Ralph Abercrombie landed with 1,500 men at Aboukir. His aim was not to occupy Egypt, but to induce
the French armies to evacuate it. He marched westward against Alexandria, keeping close to the sea. The
country on his left was very different to what it is now,
and to understand his operations two of the differences
must be remembered. (i) The "Lake of Aboukir," since
drained, stretched from Aboukir Bay almost as far as
Ramleh. As it connected with the sea, it was full of salt

water. (ii) The present Lake Mariout was almost dry. It contained a little fresh water, but most of its enormous bed was under cultivation. It lay twelve feet below the waters of Lake Aboukir, and was protected from them by a dyke. Thus Abercrombie saw water where we see land, and vice versa. He advanced with success as far as Mandourah, because his left flank was protected by Lake Aboukir. But when he wanted to attack the French position at Ramleh he feared they would outflank him over the dry bed of Mariout. His losses had been heavy, his advance was held up; wounded in the thigh by a musket shot, he had to abandon the command, and was carried on to a boat where he died; a small monument at Sidi Gaber commemorates him to-day. His successor, Hutchinson, took drastic measures. At the advice of his engineers he cut the dyke that separated Lake Aboukir from Mariout. The salt water rushed in, to the delight of the British soldiers, and in a month thousands of acres had been drowned, Alexandria was isolated from the rest of Egypt, and the left flank of the expedition was protected all the way up to the walls of the town. Later in the year a second British force landed to the west of Alexandria, at Marabout, and, caught between two fires, the French were obliged to surrender. They were given easy terms, and allowed to leave Egypt with all the honours of war. The British followed them; we had accomplished our aim, and had no reason to remain in the country any longer; we left it to our allies the Turks. But the sleep of so many centuries had been broken. The eyes of Europe were again directed to the deserted shore. Though Napoleon had failed and the British had retired, a new age had begun for Alexandria. Life flowed back into her, just as the waters, when Hutchinson cut the dyke, flowed back into Lake Mariout.

MOHAMMED ALI (1805–1848)

When Napoleon drove the Turks into the sea at Aboukir, among the fugitives was Mohammed Ali, the
founder of the present reigning house of Egypt. Little
is known of his origin. He was an Albanian, but born
at Cavala in Macedonia where he is said to have distinguished himself as a tax collector in his earlier
youth. His education was primitive; he was ignorant of
history and economics and only learnt the Arabic alphabet late in life. But he was a man of great ability
and power and an acute judge of character. He re-
appears in Egypt in 1801, still obscure, and fights under Abercrombie. When the English withdrew he prof-
ited by the internal disturbances and became in 1805
Viceroy of the country under the Sultan of Turkey.

His power was consolidated by the disastrous British
expedition of 1807—General Frazer's "reconnoitering"
expedition, as it is officially termed. England was hostile to Turkey now, and Frazer was sent to see whether
a diversion could be created in Egypt. He landed, like
Napoleon before him, at Marabout, but with no more
than the following regiments;—the 31st, the 35th, the
78th, and a foreign legion: 4,000 men in all. He occupied Alexandria and Rosetta, but before long Mohammed Ali had killed or captured half his force and

he was obliged to ask for terms. They were readily granted. The "reconnoitering" expedition was allowed to re-embark, and the only trace it has left of its presence in Alexandria is a tombstone of a soldier of the 78th, in the courtyard of the Greek Patriarchate.

For thirty years the power of Mohammed Ali grew, and with it the importance of Alexandria, his virtual capital. He freed the Holy Places of Arabia from a heretical sect, he interfered in Greece, he revolted against his suzerain the Sultan of Turkey, and invading Syria added it to his dominions. A kingdom, comparable in extent to the Ptolemaic, had come into existence with Alexandria as its centre, and it seemed that the dreams of Napoleon would be realised by this Albanian adventurer, and that the English would be cut off from India. England took alarm. And suddenly the Empire of Mohammed Ali fell. Syria revolted (1840), supported by a British fleet, and soon the English admiral, Sir Charles Napier, was at Alexandria, and compelled the Viceroy to confine himself to Egypt. According to tradition the interview took place in the new Ras-el-Tin Palace, and Napier exclaims, "If Your Highness will not listen to my unofficial appeal to you against the folly of further resistance, it only remains for me to bombard you, and by God I will bombard you and plant my bombs in the middle of this room where you are sitting." Anyhow Mohammed Ali gave in. He had failed as a European power, but he had secured for his family a comfortable principality in Egypt, where he was king in all but name.

His internal policy was rather disreputable. He admired European civilisation because it made people aggressive and gave them guns, but he had no sense of its finer aspects, and his "reforms" were mainly veneer to impress travellers. He exploited the fellahin by buying grain from them at his own price: the whole of

Egypt became his private farm. Hence the importance of the foreign communities at Alexandria at this date: he needed their aid to dispose of the produce in European markets. He won over the British and other consuls to be his agents by giving them licences to export Egyptian antiquities, which were then coming into fashion; our own Consul Henry Salt—his tomb is here —was a particular offender in this. He also gave away "Cleopatra's Needles" to the British and American Governments respectively; the obelisks that still remained on their original sites outside the vanished Caesareum, and would have lent such dignity to our modern sea front. Still, with all his faults, he did create the modern city, such as she is. He waved his wand, and what we see arose from the aged soil. Let us examine it for a moment.

THE MODERN CITY

During the years 1798–1807 as many as four expeditions had landed at or near Alexandria—one French, one Turkish, and two English. Egypt had again been drawn into the European system. A maritime capital was necessary, and the genius of Mohammed Ali realised that it could be found not in the mediaeval ports of Damietta and Rosetta, but in a restored Alexandria. The city that we know to-day has followed the lines that he laid down, and it is interesting to compare his dispositions with those of Alexander the Great, over two thousand years before.

The main problem was the waters. The English, by cutting the dykes in 1801, had refilled Lake Mariout so that it had suddenly regained its ancient area. But it was too shallow for navigation and they had filled it with salt water instead of the former fresh: it gave no access to the system of the Nile. That system had to be tapped. Alexander could find the Nile at Aboukir (Canopic Mouth): now it was as far off as Rosetta (ancient Bolbitic Mouth). Consequently Mohammed Ali had to construct a canal 45 miles long. This canal, called the Mahmoudieh after Mahmoud, the reigning Sultan of Turkey, was completed in 1820. It was badly made and the sides were always falling in, but it led to the immediate rise of Alexandria and to the decay of Rosetta. Alexandria now had water communications with Cairo, to which was added communication by rail. The Harbour followed. Mohammed Ali developed the Western which had been the less important in classical times. The present docks and arsenals were built for him (1828–1833) by the French engineer De Cerisy. A fleet was added. To the same scheme belongs the impressive Ras-el-Tin Palace, which standing on a rise above the Harbour dominated it as the Ptolemaic Palace had once dominated the Eastern; the favourite residence of the Viceroy, it indicated that his new kingdom was no mere oriental monarchy, but a modern power with its face to the sea.

Meanwhile the town started its development, but not on very regal lines. Houses began to run up and streets to sprawl over the deserted area inside the Arab Walls. It did not occur either to Mohammed Ali or to his friends the Foreign Communities that a city ought to be planned. Their one achievement was a Square and certainly quite a fine one—the Place des Consuls, now Place Mohammed Ali. The English were granted land to the north of the Square, on part of which they built their church, the French and the Greeks land to the south; areas were also acquired by other communities, *e.g.* by the Armenians. But there was no attempt to co-ordinate the various enterprises, or to utilise the existing features of the site. These features were: the sea, the lake, "Pompey's Pillar," the forts of Kom-el-Dik and Cafarelli, and the Arab Walls. The sea was ignored except for commercial purposes; the main thoroughfares still keep away from its shores, and even the fine New Quays are attracting no buildings to their curve. The lake was ignored even more completely—the lake whose delicate pale expanse might so have beautified the southern quarters; many people do not know that a lake exists. "Pompey's Pillar," instead of being the centre of converging roads, has been left where it will least be seen; only down the Rue Bab Sidra does one get a distant view of it. Similarly with the two forts; huddled behind houses. The Arab walls have been finally destroyed—remnants surviving in the eastern reach where they have been utilised (and well utilised) in the Public Gardens.

As Alexandria grew in size and wealth she required suburbs. The earliest development was along the line of the Mahmoudieh Canal, where the Villa Antoniadis and a few other fine houses have been built. But with the improvement of communications the rich merchants were able to live further afield. Two alternatives were open to them—Mex and Ramleh—and rather regrettably they selected the latter. Mex, with its fine natural features, might have developed into a very beautiful place: as it is a belt of slums have parted it from the town, and an execrable tram service has removed it even further. The town has spread to the east instead, to Ramleh, served at first by a railway and now by good electric trams.

Such are the main features of Alexandria as it has evolved under Mohammed Ali and his successors. It does not compare favourably with the city of Alexander the Great. On the other hand it is no worse than most nineteenth-century cities. And it has one immense advantage over them—a perfect climate.

THE BOMBARDMENT OF ALEXANDRIA (1882)

Thus the city develops quietly under Mohammed Ali and his successors—one of whom, Said Pasha, is buried here. Attention was rather diverted from her by the cutting of the Suez Canal, and it is not until 1882 that anything of note occurs. She is in this year connected with the rebellion of Arabi, the founder of the Egyptian Nationalist Party. Arabi, then Minister of War, was endeavouring to dominate the Khedive Tewfik, and to secure Egypt for the Egyptians. Alexandria, which had held a foreign element ever since its foundation, was therefore his natural foe, and it was here that he opened the campaign against Europe that ended in his failure at Tel-el-Kebir. The details—like Arabi's motives—are complicated. But four stages may be observed.

(i). *Riot of June 11th.*

This began at about 1.0 p.m. in the Rue des Soeurs; it is said that two donkey boys, one Arab and one Maltese, had a fight in a café, and that others joined in. The rioters moved down towards the Square, and at some cross roads near the Laban Caracol the British Consul was nearly killed. They were joined in the Square by two other mobs, one from the Attarine Quarter and one from Ras-el-Tin. British and other warships were in the harbour, but took no action, and the Egyptian troops in the city refused to intervene without orders from Arabi, who was in Cairo. At last a telegram was sent to him. He responded and the disorder ceased. There is no reason to suppose that he planned the riot. But naturally enough he used it to increase his prestige. He had shown the foreign communities, and particularly the British, that he alone could give them protection. In the evening he came down in triumph from Cairo. About 150 Europeans are thought to have been killed that day, but we have no reliable statistics.

(ii). *Bombardment of July 11th.*

British men-of-war under Admiral Seymour had been in the harbour during the riot, but it was a month before they took action. In the first place the British residents had to be removed, in the second the fleet required reinforcing, in the third orders were awaited from home. As soon as Seymour was ready he picked a quarrel with Arabi and declared he should bombard the city if any more guns were mounted in the forts.

Since Arabi would not agree he opened fire at 7.0 a.m. July 11th. There were eight iron-clads—six of them the most powerful in our navy. They were thus distributed: —*Monarch, Invincible* and *Penelope* close inshore off Mex; *Alexandria, Sultan* and *Superb* off Ras-el-Tin; while the two others the *Temeraire* and *Inflexible* were in a central position outside the harbour reef, half way between Ras-el-Tin and Marabout; and off Marabout were some gun-boats, under Lord Charles Beresford. The bombardment succeeded, though Arabi's gunners in the forts fought bravely. In the evening the *Superb* blew up the powder magazine in Fort Adda. Fort Kait Bey was also shattered and the minaret of its 15th cent. Mosque was seen "melting away like ice in the sun." The town, on the other hand, was scarcely damaged, as our gunners were careful in their aim. Arabi and his force evacuated it in the evening, marching out by the Rue Rosette to take up a position some miles further east, on the banks of the Mahmoudieh Canal.

(iii). *Riot of July 12th.*

Unfortunately Admiral Seymour, after his success, never landed a force to keep order, and the result was a riot far more disastrous than that of June. With the withdrawal of Arabi's troops the native population lost self-control. The Khedive had now broken with Arabi, but during the bombardment he had moved from Ras-el-Tin Palace to Ramleh and his authority was negligible. Pillaging went on all day on the 12th, and by the evening the city had been set on fire. The damage was material rather than artistic, the one valuable object in the Square, the statue of Mohammed Ali, fortunately escaping. Rues Chérif and Tewfik Pacha—indeed all the roads leading out of the Square—were destroyed, and nearly every street in the European quarter was impassable through fallen and falling houses. Empty jewel cases and broken clocks lay on the pavements. Every shop was looted, and by the time Admiral Seymour did land it was impossible for his middies to buy any jam; one of them has recorded this misfortune, adding that in other ways Alexandria, then in flames, was "well enough." Meanwhile the Khedive had returned to his Palace, and order was slowly restored. It is not known how many lives were lost in this avoidable disaster.

(iv). *Military Operations.*

A large British force was despatched under Lord Wolseley to the Suez Canal—the force that finally defeated Arabi at Tel-el-Kebir. But, until it reached Egypt, Alexandria remained in danger, for Arabi might attack from his camp at Kafr-el-Dawar. So the city had to be defended on the east. In the middle of July General Alison arrived with a few troops, including artillery, and occupied the barracks at Mustapha Pacha, the hill of Abou-el-Nawatir, and the water works down by the canal. He could thus watch Arabi's movements. And he had a second strongly fortified position at the gates of the Antoniadis Gardens, in case he was attacked from the south. Here he was able to hold on and to harry the enemy's outposts until pressure was relieved. His losses were slight; the regiments involved are commemorated by tablets in the English church. Next month Wolseley arrived, and having inspected the position re-embarked his troops and pretended that he was going to land at Aboukir. Arabi was deceived and prepared resistance there. Wolseley steamed past him, and landed at Port Said instead. Arabi then had to break up his camp, and the danger for Alexandria was over.

CONCLUSION

Since the bombardment of 1882, the city has known other troubles, but they will not be here described. Nor will any peroration be attempted, for the reason that Alexandria is still alive and alters even while one tries to sum her up. Politically she is now more closely connected with the rest of Egypt than ever in the past, but the old foreign elements remain, and it is to the oldest of them, the Greek, that she owes such modern culture as is to be found in her. Her future like that of other great commercial cities is dubious. Except in the cases of the Public Gardens and the Museum, the Municipality has scarcely risen to its historic responsibilities. The Library is starved for want of funds, the Art Gallery cannot be alluded to, and links with the past have been wantonly broken—for example the name of the Rue Rosette has been altered and the exquisite Covered Bazaar near the Rue de France destroyed. Material prosperity based on cotton, onions, and eggs, seems assured, but little progress can be discerned in other directions, and neither the Pharos of Sostratus nor the Idylls of Theocritus nor the Enneads of Plotinus are likely to be rivalled in the future. Only the climate, only the north wind and the sea remain as pure as when Menelaus, the first visitor, landed upon Ras-el-Tin, three thousand years ago; and at night the constellation of Berenice's Hair still shines as brightly as when it caught the attention of Conon the astronomer.

THE GOD ABANDONS ANTONY

When at the hour of midnight
an invisible choir is suddenly heard passing
with exquisite music, with voices—
Do not lament your fortune that at last subsides,
your life's work that has failed, your schemes that have
    proved illusions.
But like a man prepared, like a brave man,
bid farewell to her, to Alexandria who is departing.
Above all, do not delude yourself, do not say that it is a
    dream,
that your ear was mistaken.
Do not condescend to such empty hopes.
Like a man for long prepared, like a brave man,
like to the man who was worthy of such a city,
go to the window firmly,
and listen with emotion,
but not with the prayers and complaints of the coward
(Ah! supreme rapture!)
listen to the notes, to the exquisite instruments of the
    mystic choir,
and bid farewell to her, to Alexandria whom you are
    losing.

C. P. CAVAFY.*

* The local reference of this exquisite poem is to the omen that
heralded the defeat of Mark Antony (p. 29). The poet is eminent
among the contemporary writers of Greece; he and his translator,
Mr. George Valassopoulo, are both residents of Alexandria.
[Cavafy died in 1933.]

PART II
GUIDE

MEDITERRANEAN

PREHISTORIC HARBOUR

ISLAND OF

[Ras el Tin]

TEMPLE OF POSEIDON

CATACOMBS (of Anfouchy)

EUNOSTOS HARBOUR

Present Coastline

DOCKS

GATE OF THE MOON

† CH. OF ST. THEONAS

[Gabbari]

[Arab

CANAL

WESTERN

CEMETERY

TEMPLE OF SERAPIS
POMPEY'S PILLAR
LIBRARY

R H

CATACOMBS [Kom el Chogafa]

CANAL FOLLOWING

PROBABLE

LAKE MAREOTIS

ALEXANDRIA
HISTORICAL MAP

Ancient Sites in CAPITALS
Modern Sites bracketed [ ]

SEA

PHAROS·LIGHTHOUSE
[Fort Kait Bey]

PHAROS

TEMPLE OF
ISIS ON PHAROS

☐ TIMONIUM

GREAT HARBOUR

ROYAL HARBOUR

CAPE LOCHIAS
(Silsileh)
TEMPLE OF ISIS

HEPTASTADION DYKE

Present Coastline

Place
[mohammed Ali]

ISLAND PALACE

ST.
ANTIRRHODOS

AREA OF PALACE

CH. OF
ST. MARK

Cleopatra's
Needles
CAESAREUM
THEATRE

+ CONVENT OF ST.
CATHERINE
CH. OF ST.
ATHANASIUS

RACE
COURSE
(Arab Walls)

(Chatby)

JEWISH
QUARTER

CANOPIC STREET

AREA OF MOUSEION
LIBRARY SOMA

[Now Rue Rosette]

GATE OF
THE SUN
TO CANOPUS

SHRINE OF
POMPEY

Walls of A.D. 811

PARK OF PAN

(Porte Rosette)

AKOTIS

RACE
COURSE

STREET OF THE SOMA
[Now Rue Nebi Daniel]

COURSE

OF MAHMOUDIEH

COURSE

OF WALLS B.C. 331

Lake Harbour

CANAL

TO CANOPUS
AND NILE

EASTERN CEMETERIES

[Lake Mariout]

SECTION I

From the Square to the Rue Rosette

ROUTE:—Square, Rue Chérif Pacha, Rue Rosette, leading through the most modern section of the town. No tram line.

CHIEF POINTS OF INTEREST:—Square and Statue of Mohammed Ali; Banco di Roma; Mosque of the Prophet Daniel; St. Saba; Greco-Roman Museum.

THE SQUARE

The Square (officially, Place Mohammed Ali; formerly Place des Consuls; known to cabmen as "Menschieh" from the adjoining Police Station) was laid out by Mohammed Ali as the centre of his new city. (About 1830; *see* p. 97). In Ptolemaic times the ground here was under the sea. The Square is over 100 yds. broad and nearly 500 long and well planted, but unworthy buildings surround it. It suffered in the riots of 1882 (p. 101); everything was then burnt excepting the statue of Mohammed Ali and the Church of St. Mark.

In the Centre:—*Equestrian Statue of Mohammed Ali,* an impressive specimen of French Sculpture, by Jacquemart; exhibited in the Salon of 1872. Orthodox Mohammedans were hostile to its erection, and even now there is no inscription on it. Its presence is the more welcome since it is one of the few first class objects in the city. It should be studied from every point of view.

Right as one faces the Statue:—*The Mixed Tribunals,* where, in accordance with arrangements dating from 1875, civil and commercial cases between Egyptians and Europeans are tried.

Left:—*The French Gardens,* a pleasant strip, stretching at right angles from the Square to the New Quays, (p. 153).

Also left:—*Anglican Church of St. Mark,* which with the adjacent St. Mark's Buildings was built on land granted to the English by Mohammed Ali. Looking through the railings of the churchyard is the funny little bust of General Earle (k. 1885 at Kirbekan in the Soudan). It was erected by the European Community, and represents their chief incursion into the realms of art. The Church itself, considering its date (1855), and its pseudo-Byzantine architecture, is however a tolerable building. The interior is restful and the stained glass and triptych in the chancel strike a pleasing note of colour. Historically, its only associations are with the fighting against Arabi in 1882 (p. 99). The Regiments it commemorates are the 2nd Bn. Duke of Cornwall's Light Infantry (on the scroll by the entrance stairs); 2nd Bn. Derbyshires; Royal Marine Artillery; 1st Bn. London Division; Royal Artillery 1st Bn. Royal West Kents (in the Nave). In the churchyard trees multitudinous, sparrows gather at sunset, and fill the Square with their chatter.

End of the Square:—*The Bourse,* with arcaded exterior and clock. Inside is the Cotton Exchange, the chief in the Egyptian trade; the howls and cries that may be heard here of a morning proceed not from a menagerie but from the wealthy merchants of Alexandria as they buy and sell. At the other end of the same hall is the Stock Exchange. The whole scene is well worth a visit (introduction necessary).

Rue Chérif Pacha, a smart little street bristling with flag staffs, leads out of the Square to the left of the Bourse. Here are the best shops. Towards the end, left, at the entrance of the Rue Toussoum Pacha, is the *Banco di Roma,* the finest building in the city. Architect, Gorra. A modified copy of the famous Palazzo Farnese, which Antonio da San Gallo and Michelangelo built in the 16th cent., at Rome. The materials are artificial stone and narrow bricks of a charming pale red. It has two stories as against the Farnese's three, but there is a sort of half storey up under the heavy cornice. Each side of the door are elaborate torch holders of bent iron; over door, the Wolf of Rome. In a cosmopolitan city like Alexandria, which has never evolved an architecture of its own, there is nothing incongruous in this copy of the Italian Renaissance. A little further up Rue Toussoum Pacha is the *Land Bank of Egypt,* with a good semicircular portico.

Rue Chérif Pacha then joins the Rue Rosette.

RUE ROSETTE

This street, despite its modern appearance, is the most ancient in the city. It runs on the lines of the Canopic Way, the central artery of Alexander's town, (p. 10), and under the Ptolemies it was lined from end to end with marble colonnades. Its full title is "Rue de la Porte Rosette" from the Rosetta Gate in the old Arab walls through which it passed out eastwards (p. 86). The Municipality have recently changed its name to

the unmeaning Rue Fouad Premier, thus breaking one
of the few links that bound their city to the past.

At its entrance, right, are:—the Caracol Attarine
(British Main Guard); the Rue de la Gare du Caire,
leading to the main railway station; and the Mohammed Ali Club, the chief in the town—a small temple
to Serapis once stood on its site. Here too is Cook's
office.

100 yds. down it is crossed by the Rue Nebi Daniel
and by a tramway. Here, in ancient times, was the
main crossway of the ancient city—one of the most glorious places in the world (p. 10). Achilles Tatius, a
bishop who in A.D. 400 wrote a somewhat foolish and
improper novel called Clitophon and Leucippe, thus
describes it:—

> The first thing one noticed in entering Alexandria by
> the Gate of the Sun (i.e. by the Rosetta Gate) was the
> beauty of the city. A range of columns went from one
> end of it to the other. Advancing down them, I came in
> time to the place that bears the name of Alexander, and
> there could see the other half of the town, which was
> equally beautiful. For just as the colonnades stretched
> ahead of me, so did other colonnades now appear at right
> angles to them.

Thus the tramway was also lined with marble once.

Turning to the right, a few yards up the Rue Nebi
Daniel, we come to:—*The Mosque of the Prophet
Daniel* which stands on the site of Alexander's tomb—
the "Soma" where he and some of the Ptolemies lay,
buried in the Macedonian fashion (p. 22). The cellars
have never been explored, and there is a gossipy story
that Alexander still lies in one of them, intact: a drago-
man from the Russian Consulate, probably a liar, said
in 1850 that he saw through a hole in a wooden door
"a human body in a sort of glass cage with a diadem on
its head and half bowed on a sort of elevation or throne.

A quantity of books or papyrus were scattered around."
The present Mosque, though the chief in the city, is
uninteresting; a paved approach, a whitewashed door,
a great interior supported by four colonnades with
slightly pointed arches. The praying niche faces south
instead of the usual east. All has been mercilessly restored. Stairs lead down to two tombs, assigned to the
Prophet Daniel and to the mythical Lukman the Wise;
it is uncertain why or when such a pair visited our city.
The tombs stand in a well-crypt of cruciform shape,
above which is a chapel roofed by a dome and entered from the Mosque through a door. Here and there
some decorations struggle through the whitewash.

In a building to the right of the approach to the
Mosque are the *Tombs of the Khedivial Family,* worth
seeing for their queerness; there is nothing like them in
Alexandria. The Mausoleum is cruciform, painted to
imitate marble, and covered with Turkey carpets. Out
of the carpet rise the tombs, of all sizes but of similar
design, and all painted white and gold. A red tarboosh
indicates a man, a crown with conventionalised hair a
woman. The most important person buried here is Said
Pacha—third tomb on the right. He was the son of Mohammed Ali and ruled Egypt 1854–1863: Mohammed
Ali himself lies at Cairo.

Between the Mausoleum and the street:—a fountain
with eaves and a dome; Turkish style.

Opposite the Mosque:—some antique columns used
as gate posts; perhaps the façade of the Mouseion
stretched along here (p. 19).

Behind the Mosque:—Fort of Kom-el-Dik. View.
Site of ancient Paneum or Park of Pan—the summit of
the hill was then carved into a pinecone, which a
spiral path ascended.—In Arab times the walls of the
shrunken city passed to the south of Kom-el-Dik, (p.
86), and a fine stretch of them still survives, half way

between the base of the Fort and the railway station; they border the road, but cannot be seen from it, being sunken; they include a moat.—Beyond the Fort the high ground continues; the little Arab quarter of Kom-el-Dik is built along its crest, and the winding lanes, though insignificant, contrast pleasantly with the glare of the European town.

We return to the Rue Rosette.

A little further down the Rue Rosette a turning on the left leads to the *Church and Convent of St. Saba*, the seat of the Greek Orthodox Patriarch. (For history of Patriarchate, *see* p. 227.) A church was founded here in 615, on the site of a Temple of Apollo. The present group dates from 1687, and has an old world atmosphere that is rare in Alexandria. In the quiet court of the Convent are three tombstones of British soldiers, dating from Napoleonic times: Colonel Arthur Brice of the Coldstreams, k. in the Battle of Alexandria, 1801 (p. 93); Thomas Hamilton Scott of the 78th, and Henry Gosle, military apothecary, who both died during General Frazer's disastrous "reconnoitering" expedition, 1807, (p. 94).—From the court, steps descend to the church which has been odiously restored. In the nave, eight ancient columns of granite, now smeared with chocolate paint. In the apse of the sanctuary, fresco of the Virgin and Child. Right—Chapel of St. George with a table said to be 4th cent., and an interesting picture of the Council of Nicaea (p. 53); the Emperor Constantine presides with the bishops around him and the heretic Arius at his feet. Left—Chapel of St. Catherine of Alexandria, with a block of marble purporting to come from the column where the saint was martyred.—Hanging outside the church, three fine bells.

At the top of the street, to left, is the Greek Hospital, a pleasant building that stands in a garden.

The Rue Rosette now passes the Native Courts (left) and reaches the Municipal Buildings. Behind the latter, a few yards up the Rue du Musée, is the Municipal Library; go up the steps opposite the entrance gate; push the door. The Library is good considering its miserable endowment; the city that once had the greatest Library in the world now cannot afford more than £300 per annum for the combined purchase and binding of her books.

Beyond the Library is a far more adequate institution—the Greco-Roman Museum.

THE GRECO-ROMAN MUSEUM

The collection was not formed until 1891, by which time most of the antiques in the neighbourhood had passed into private hands. It is consequently not of the first order and little in it has outstanding beauty. Used rightly, it is of great value, but the visitor who "goes through" it will find afterwards that it has gone through him, and that he is left with nothing but a vague memory of fatigue. The absence of colour, the numerous small exhibits in terra cotta and limestone, will tend to depress him, and to give a false impression of a civilisation which, whatever its defects, was not dull. He should not visit the collection until he has learned or imagined something about the ancient city, and he should visit certain definite objects, and then come away—a golden rule indeed in all museums. He may then find that a scrap of the past has come alive.

The collection is well housed (date of building 1895) and well catalogued. There is a Guide (in French) by the Director, Professor Breccia, extracts from which are pasted up about the rooms. On this scholarly work

PLAN OF GRECO-ROMAN MUSEUM

the following notes are based. They are compiled, however, from a particular point of view. They attempt to illustrate the historical section of the book (p. 5), and are connected with it by cross references.

For arrangement of exhibits, *see* Plan opposite.

INTRODUCTION

The Museum mainly illustrates the civilisation of Ancient Alexandria. There are some portraits—not satisfactory—of the Founder (Room 12), and magnificent coins of the Ptolemies (Room 3); also sculptures of them (Rooms 4, 12). Their religious policy appears in the statues of Serapis (Room 16). As for the Roman Emperors, we have besides their coins (Room 2) colossal statues of Marcus Aurelius (Room 12), and of Diocletian (?) (Room 17); then some gold coins of their Byzantine successors (Room 5). Meanwhile the career of the private citizen is also being illustrated, but mainly in his grave. Masses and masses and masses of funerary stuff (Rooms 6, 13–15, 17–21), mostly dull, but attaining great beauty in the terra cotta statuettes of women (Room 18). The "Egyptian Queen" pottery (Room 17) is more cheerful. In the same room is lovely glass. With Christianity, the Alexandrian, though still mainly presented to us through his tombs (Room 1), develops the interesting cult of St. Menas (Rooms 1, 5, 22A).

The Museum also exhibits, though imperfectly, other aspects of Egyptian life.

(i). PHARAONIC EGYPT:—There are some mummies, etc., from Thebes, Heliopolis, etc. (Rooms 8 and 10), but they have the air of being here because not good enough for Cairo; also a collection of small objects (Room 10), and Rameses statues from Aboukir (Room

9 and North Garden). The blend of Pharaonic and Hellenistic is shown in Room 11.

(ii). THE FAYOUM:—This is the most important non-Alexandrian section in the Museum. The Fayoum, an irrigated depression south-west of Cairo, was developed by Ptolemy II Philadelphus, and, as in Alexandria, Greek and Egyptian mingled, but with different results. It was barbaric and provincial. Note especially crocodile worship (North Garden, Rooms 9, 22A). Mummies of quite a new type (Room 17). Black basalt statues (Room 11). It is a pity that the Fayoum exhibits cannot all be shown together.

(iii). AKHMIN:—An early Christian Necropolis in Upper Egypt. Hence come the robed mummies (Room 1), and the fragments of tapestry (Rooms 1, 2, 4), whose beauty will linger when many a grandiose statue has been forgotten.

VESTIBULE.

PLANS, PHOTOGRAPHS, ETC.

Note especially (1) Thiersch's reconstruction of the Pharos and (10) photographs of Kait Bey Fort, where the Pharos stood (p. 18). (8) Cleopatra's Needle in situ (p. 175). At the entrance of Room 6 (left) is a cast of the Rosetta Stone (p. 199) which contains a tri-lingual decree (Hieroglyph, which was the script of the Ancient Egyptian priests, Demotic, a running hand-writing evolved from it, and Greek); the decree was passed by the priests of Memphis, B.C. 196, in honour of Ptolemy V Epiphanes. The original stone was discovered by the French in 1799 in the Fort of St. Julien, Rosetta—water-colour of it hangs close by. General Menou had to surrender it to the English in 1801, and it is now in the British Museum. Carducci's fine poem on Alexandria hangs framed on the adjacent wall.

In the case are stone-age tools from the Fayoum.

From the Vestibule are: right, Room 1 (Christianity);

left, Room 6 (Inscriptions); straight ahead, the Verandah leads between the Garden Courts to Room 17.

ROOM 1: CHRISTIAN REMAINS.

RIGHT WALL: Inscriptions. 106 shows a cross with a looped top, directly derived from the symbol of life (ankh) that the ancient Egyptian gods carry (p. 74). In the middle of the wall *Case A:* terra cotta dolls, etc., from St. Menas.

CENTRE OF ROOM, facing door:—magnificent Byzantine capital, supposed to have been in the church of St. Mark (p. 50). Found in the Rue Ramleh. *Case K:* Carved ivories and bones, mostly from Alexandrian rubbish heaps—1979, 2012, 2021, 2025 are good examples. *Case I:* Interlaced cushion from the Christian necropolis of Antinoe, Upper Egypt. Middle of room: fine porphyry cover to a sarcophagus, decorated on each side by a charming head. From the Lebban quarter. Beyond: Christian mummies from Antinoe, still wearing their fine embroideries. At the end: another Byzantine capital, found near the Mahmoudieh Canal.

LEFT WALL, centre: *Cases La* and *M:* Flasks from St. Menas. They were filled with water, which must soon have evaporated, and exported all over the Christian world: usual design—the Saint between camels. Between the vases interesting fragments from a church to St. Menas at Dekhela (p. 185); the bas-relief of the Saint is a clumsy copy of the one that stood in his shrine in the desert (p. 210). *Cases P, Q, R, S:* Coptic tapestries from Akhmin and Antinoe—beautiful. Date 3rd cent. onward. Near *Case N*, two absurd reliefs (Christian era) of Leda and the swan —in one of them she holds an egg.

ROOM 2: COINS.

Chronological continuation of the Ptolemaic coins in Room 3, which should be visited first. Illustrate history of Alexandria, and also her religion, under Rome and afterwards under Constantinople. Series begins in *Case A* (further right-hand corner) with Octavian (Augustus) 675; *Case B*, No. 675 (of Domitian) shows the Pharos (*see*

p. 18). 750 (of Trajan)—a temple to Isis in Alexandria, with pylons between which the goddess stands. 771 shows Serapis on his throne. 890–892, the sacred basket that he sometimes carries on his head. *Case C*, 1363–1366—interviews, very friendly, between the Emperor Hadrian and Alexandria. 1409—interviews between him and the god Serapis. 1450, Isis as guardian of the Pharos.

ROUND THE ROOM: Four marble capitals from St. Menas.

ROOM 3: COINS.

The collection of Ptolemaic coins begins in *Case Ab* (right of room) and continues through *Case C–D* (left) and *Case E–F* (entrance). The coins are numbered consecutively. They are of great historical and artistic interest, but must not be taken seriously as portraits, since the ruler is generally approximated to some god (*i.e.* numeral "one" 1). Silver four-drachma of Alexander the Great, struck by his Viceroy Cleomenes. 2–45. Ptolemy I as Viceroy. On the obverse is always the head of Alexander the Great, with horns of the God Ammon. 46–274. Ptolemy I as King (Soter). A new type gradually appears; on the obverse the head of the King, on the reverse an eagle (note 14 gold coins—four-drachma pieces). 275–510. Ptolemy II (Philadelphus) instructive for the domestic history of his reign (p. 16). At first the King appears alone—*e.g.* on gold five-drachma. 275–280. Then his formidable sister and wife Arsinoe is alone—gold coin 342. Then the couple appear together—gold 428–434, while on the other side of the coins are their predecessors, Ptolemy I and his wife, to show that the dynasty emanated in pairs. 551–619. Ptolemy III (Euergetes). 620. Magnificent gold eight-drachma, representing Euergetes, but struck by Philopator his son; the most gorgeous coin in the collection. 621. Silver four-drachma, with heads of Serapis and Isis. Ptolemaic coinage now deteriorates; the eagle in the later issues (*Case D*) becomes formalised and ridiculous. 1059 (*Case E*) features —what disillusionment!—Cleopatra!

ROUND THE ROOM: Casts.

ROOM 4: COINS: AKHMIN TAPESTRY.

The coins are coppers of the later Roman Emperors.
Not beautiful. Of historical interest to Alexandria. In *Case
A–B* (right) 3884–Aurelian and Vabatathe. 3896–Zeno-
bia. In *Case C–D* (left) 4024–Diocletian.

ROUND THE WALLS: 1–8. Tapestries from the Christian
cemetery at Akhmin.

BACK WALL: Large and impressive statue of a mourning
woman with her child. Hellenistic. Perhaps represents
Berenice wife of Ptolemy III Euergetes, mourning for her
little daughter—the daughter whom the priests deified in
the Decree of Canopus, B.C. 239 (p. 46).

ENTRANCE OF ROOM: Large Christian Jar.

ROOM 5: COINS.

Beautiful Byzantine gold coins. Note especially the Emperor Phocas and his conqueror Heraclius (p. 58); the latter displays the Exaltation of the Cross, recovered by him
from the Persians.

BACK WALL: Pilaster from the Hospice at St. Menas.
The cross has been erased, probably at the Arab conquest.
At each end of it, more St. Menas flasks.

Case A: Painted masks, from the (pagan) Necropolis of
Antinoe. *Case B;* Christian potteries from Kom es Chogafa.

Return to Vestibule.

ROOM 6: INSCRIPTIONS, ETC.

This room contains nothing of beauty, but is interesting
historically. The exhibits are not in numerical order.

RIGHT WALL, close to entrance: 42—Inscription on a
statue of Antony (p. 28), dedicated on December 24th,
B.C. 50 (Found near Ramleh Station, *i.e.* the site of the
Caesareum). 2. Dedication to Ptolemy II Philadelphus.
1. Dedication to Ptolemy I. 37. Doorway with inscription
to Ptolemy VI; in it is a case containing (59) two bronze
plaques belonging to a Roman soldier, (Julius Saturninus),
inscribed with a certificate of his good services and privi-
leges. 61*a,* also in the case, is another military document,

a wooden tablet written at Alexandria, but found in the Fayoum, and also conferring benefits on a veteran. 94. Base of a statue of the Emperor Valentinian (4th cent. A.D.); found in Rue Rosette. 88b. Tombstone with the figures of Isidore and Artemisia, two ladies of Pisidia, found at Hadra. 87b. Tombstone of a lady with her servant.

Then come some painted tombstones protected by glass; they are inferior to some in the rooms further on. 119 (in corner of room); Tombstone of a woman expiring between two friends.

LEFT WALL: Inscriptions and tombstones of the Roman period (p. 48). 480. On a pedestal: Memorial of Aurelius Alexander, a Roman soldier of Macedonian birth who died aged 31. 252. Another of Aurelius Sabius, a Syrian soldier, aged 35.

EACH SIDE OF THE ROOM, near entrance door: Two *Cases* of papyri—the left hand one containing two interesting inscriptions. 119. Incantation to the Nile and to the great spirit Sabaoth shewing mixture of Egyptian and Jewish faiths. 122. Demand of Aurelia, priestess of the crocodile god, Petesouchos, for a certificate of having worshipped the gods. It was made during the Decian persecution, (p. 50), and suggests that, despite her position, she had been accused of Christianity. 352b. On a pedestal: Colossal scarab. 35b. Fine headless sphinx. 351. Great Apis bull (restored); period of Hadrian. 350. Sphinx, rather sentimental, with crossed paws. All these last four were found near "Pompey's Pillar" (p. 157).

ROOM 7: ANCIENT EGYPT: CANOPUS.

These monuments, though mostly found in the Aboukir sites (p. 190), may have been imported there at some unknown date from Heliopolis or Sais.

1. Statue of a Hyksos Pharaoh (Shepherd King, about B.C. 1800) which has been appropriated by Rameses II (B.C. 1300); on the shoulder appears Rameses' daughter Hout-Ma-Ra, traditionally the princess who found Moses in the bullrushes.

18. Part of a statue of Rameses II.

Case C (left of room). Two statues of a Ptolemaic official; from the Temple of Serapis, Alexandria (p. 161).

ROOM 8: ANCIENT EGYPT.

Five mummy cases.

Case B (right): The interior is painted—an eerie receptacle. By the head, a winged serpent; along the sides, a serpent with the sign of Life (cf. the Coptic Cross, Room 1, No. 106, also p. 74), and genii, mostly serpent-headed. The mummy lay on the sun-goddess Neith, on a serpent entwined round a lotus, and on the soul as a bird. The outside of the case is also painted. From Deir el Bahri, Upper Egypt.

Case E (centre): Richly painted mummy with the goddess Neith on its breast. Very effective. Date—about B.C. 600.

3 (back wall): Relief from over the door of a tomb. Left, the deceased, enthroned between two bouquets of lotus; to one of them a couple of ducks are tied. Then comes an old harpist, who is singing, accompanied by a girl on a drum, and by two others who clap their hands. To the right, a man preparing drink; then two dancing girls. Beautiful work. From Heliopolis.

ROOM 9: ANCIENT EGYPT: CROCODILE WORSHIP.

The contents of this room, though not Alexandrian, are Ptolemaic, and well illustrate that dynasty in its Egyptian aspect. They come from the Temple of Petesouchos, the crocodile god of the Fayoum. The temple was adorned by Agathodorus, a Greek official there B.C. 137, in honour of Ptolemy VII (Physkon) and of his two wives, one his sister, one his niece, and both called Cleopatra. (For the marriage arrangements of this unattractive monarch, *see* tree, p. 14). The temple itself has been in part brought to the Museum, and well set up in the North Garden, (*see* below).

CENTRE OF ROOM: Wooden stretcher on which is mummied crocodile. It was carried thus in procession by the priests, as the water colour below (copy of a fresco) shows. The stretcher rests on a wooden chest, also found in the shrine.

BACK WALL: Wooden door of the outer gateway (*see* North Garden). Greek inscription. Here are some photographs by which the temple can be reconstructed.

39 (right of the chest): An offering table to the god, ornate and unpleasing. He lies in a little tank.

LEFT OF THE ENTRANCE DOOR: Relief of a priest adoring the god, who crawls upon lotus flowers.

ROOM 10: ANCIENT EGYPT: SMALL EXHIBITS.

IN THE ENTRANCE: Offering table, with basins for the libations.

RIGHT WALL: *Case C;* Statuettes of gods, all named. The most interesting for the history of Alexandria are 3–25 Osiris, and 26–40 the bull Apis, with whom he was compounded to make Serapis (p. 21).

Case D: Mummies of a baby, of an eagle, of an ibis.

Case Aa—Shelf b (at the top): Winged scarabs in blue enamel. *Shelf k* (No. 1): statuette of Sekhet, goddess of the heat of the sun—she has the head of a lioness and holds a gold flower. *Shelf f:* Bast, the cat-god. No. 39 has a kitten between the paws. 51. Gold earrings. *Shelf* 1 has more statues of Bast. 55. Very good.

LEFT WALL: *Case H;* "Canopic" vases of alabaster. Used to hold those parts of the dead that could not be embalmed. Each dedicated to a son of Horus. Amset held the stomach; Hapi the intestines; Douamoutef the lungs; Kebehsenouf the liver. For their connection with the town of Canopus, *see* p. 190.

*Case Bb:—*More statuettes—especially *Shelf i.—*Harpocrates and Horus; and *Shelf k,* Isis nursing Horus—the artistic origin for the Christian design of the Madonna and Child (p. 74). There are some rattles and vases of the Isis cult.

Case L: Little serving figures (Ushabti), which were put in the grave with the mummy to do the work for it in the underworld.

Also round the wall of the room: six painted mummy cases.

Down the middle: two big tables of scarabs, amulets, gold trinkets, etc.

ROOM 11: GRECO-EGYPTIAN.

Objects in which the Greek and Egyptian influences mingle. They are few in number, and not as interesting as one might expect. No living art was born from the union.

RIGHT WALL: 18. Dedication to the Egyptian god Anubis with a Greek inscription. 20. Profile of a Ptolemy—rather charming. 33–40. Serpent worship—very repulsive. 40 is a curious mixture. The male snake has the basket of Serapis and the club of Hercules; the female, the disc of Isis and the sheaf of Ceres. 41. Bad painting, Greek style, of a girl with Egyptian gods round her. From Gabbari.

END WALL (both sides): 43–53. Clumsy statues from the Fayoum, in which Greek influence appears.

LEFT WALL (centre): 61. Large fragment of a relief from a temple at Benha; left, Horus with a falcon's head; right, a human figure, by whose side is a Greek inscription. 62. Model of a shrine, mixed style: in the sanctuary Isis nurses Horus. 69. (in *Case* A)—beautiful statue (headless) of a woman, Egyptian style, but Greek feeling.

Archway between Rooms 11 and 12. ON RIGHT: Portrait of a youth in white marble (from Kom es Chogafa). LEFT: Pleasing portrait of a child of two or three years of age.

ROOM 12: PORTRAITS: MOSTLY GRECO-ROMAN IN STYLE.

CENTRE: 30. Dull colossal statue of Marcus Aurelius. The Emperor, looking bored but benignant, appears as a general: his right arm rests on a cornucopia. A cross has in Christian times been scratched on the stomach of the cuirass.—From Rue Rosette.

RIGHT WALL: 8. Exquisite bust of Venus; 16a and 17. Heads, in marble and granite, of Alexander the Great (p. 8); of no artistic merit; but found in Alexandria. 18. Head of a young soldier. 20. Marble head of a goddess; beautiful hair. Found near "Pompey's Pillar." 21. Head, perhaps of

Berenice, wife of Euergetes; found in same place.—*Cabinet A:* Small portraits: note as especially fine 15 and 15*a* Ptolemy Euergetes (?) and 12 Berenice his wife (?) with elaborate curls; they stand in the centre of the case on the second shelf. *Cabinet D:* Alleged portrait in marble of Cleopatra in her declining years. Thin, firmly compressed lips and general expression of severity discredit the theory. 60. Colossal granite head of Ptolemy IV Philopator; from Aboukir.

LEFT WALL: 51. Bust of Emperor Hadrian. 52. Head in white marble—noble features, supposed to be those of Marcus Aurelius in youth. *Cabinet B:* Heads and torsos: No. 27 (centre shelf), Head of a child with radiant smile— found in Alexandria. 36. Head of Zeus, hirsute countenance—thick lips. Has been scalped. *Cabinet F:* Various small bronzes; 44. Life-sized head of woman in marble: has Rosetti-like neck and mouth.

ROOM 13: MISCELLANEOUS.

CENTRE: 1. Statue of an Emperor, on which a head of Septimus Severus has been fixed.

In *Case F* (right): 2. Smiling face of a Faun. On the top of the case, a queer relief of a winged griffin and a woman on two wheels. (Nemesis ?).

In *Case H* (left): 2. Caricature of a Roman senator with a rat's head.

ROOM 14: MISCELLANEOUS.

CENTRE: Mosaic from Gabbari, once displaying a Medusa's head.

BACK WALL: 1. Marble statue of a Roman orator. The head does not belong.

LEFT CORNER: 2–4. Delicate architectural details. From Rue Sultan Hussein.

LEFT WALL: 6. Door of a tomb-niche, blending Greek and Egyptian styles. The table in front is from the same tomb and was used for funeral offering. From the Western Necropolis.

ROOM 15: ARCHITECTURAL.

Small fragments, etc., many of them very dainty and showing traces of paint.

RIGHT WALL: 9. Sacrificial altar, imitating a building, with doors realistically ajar.

On a column in the right-hand corner: 2. Capital, well illustrating mixture of styles; the general form and the acanthus leaves are Greek, the lotus, papyrus, and serpents are Egyptian.

MIDDLE WALL, behind a curtain: 20. Painted side of a sarcophagus; a shallow and pretty design of two gamecocks about to fight across a festoon of flowers. 2nd cent. A.D.

LEFT WALL: 50. Other side of same sarcophagus; buildings in perspective.

ROOM 16: STATUES, MOSTLY GRECO-ROMAN IN STYLE.

RIGHT WALL: 4. Marble torso of a young hero or god; the head and arms, which were worked separately, are lost, good work. From Alexandria—probably on a temple. 7–8. *On a shelf*—Statuettes, headless and insignificant, but interesting for their subject:—Alexander the Great as a god with the aegis. From Alexandria. 12. On a column—Bust of the composite-goddess Demeter-Selene, showing head-dress of Demeter and horns of the moon. 21–23: Priestesses of Isis, recognisable by the sacred knots into which their shawls are tied in front. 28. Large Ionic capital; another stands opposite, four others in the garden court. From Silsileh, and is probably part of the Ptolemaic Palace (p. 18). 27. Greek funeral relief, as old as 3rd cent. B.C. Found at Alexandria, but probably imported from Athens.

CENTRE OF ROOM: 31. Fine bath of black stone, decorated with heads of lions and of a lynx, through whom the water escaped. Further on (37) is another. Both from the Western Necropolis, where they were used as tombs. 33. Colossal votive foot, merging above the ankle into a bust of Serapis. On the head a Greek dedication to Serapis from two of his worshippers; two serpents above with a child (Horus ?) between them. From Alexandria. 34. An immense eagle, rather cumbersome, and presented by the late

Khedive; from the island of Thasos. 39. Gigantic forearm, holding a sphere. From Benha.

LEFT WALL: 40. Big limestone Corinthian capital. 3rd cent. B.C. 47, 48, 49, 51, and (*on shelf*) 53 and 52*a*: Statues and Heads of Serapis. Important (p. 21). 47 is probably a Roman copy of the original—ascribed to Bryaxis —in the Temple, and well renders the type—half terrible half benign. On its head are the marks where the sacred basket was attached. From the Rue Adib. 48 shows Cerberus. 52 and 52*a* were found near the actual Serapeum; the blue-black colour of the latter recalls the original statue. 50. Priest of Serapis (?) headless; robe with seven-rayed stars, scarabs, the crescent moon. Apis Bulls and a great serpent. From the Temple. 53. Realistic Portrait head. 54. Apollo seated on the Omphalos, or Navel of the World at Delphi; a rare subject; probably imported from Antioch, Asia Minor. 59. Headless statues, Roman, some with rolls of papyrus by them. From Sidi Gaber. 62. Entrance of Room 17: Genius of Death asleep.

ROOM 17: MISCELLANEOUS.

An interesting room.

CENTRE: Delightful mosaic of a water party in Upper Egypt; birds, frogs, eels, fish, hippopotami and pigmies; in the middle a lady and gentleman with their offspring and an attendant recline beneath an awning that sways in the wind. Caesar and Cleopatra may have disported themselves thus (p. 27). Greek inscription and ornamental border.

BACK WALL: Colossal headless porphyry statue of Diocletian (?) on a throne. From Rue Attarine.

IN FRONT OF STATUE: Marble sarcophagus; Dionysus and Ariadne. From the Western Necropolis. The type is rare in Alexandria, the decorations being generally fruit or flowers.

PLACED ABOUT THE ROOM: Mummies from the Fayoum (*see* preliminary note); the best (*Case U*) stands against a pillar; it has a realistic portrait of the deceased, painted on wood.

ROUND THE WALLS: *Case A:* Lovely iridescent glass; the

Alexandrian glass was famous. *Case D,* terra cotta dish for serving poached eggs. *Table Rr:* Funerary objects from the Western Necropolis; 2506, &c., Gnostic Amulets (p. 75). *Case G* and adjoining *Table S:* Fragments of "Egyptian Queen" pottery, a commercial product of Ptolemaic times. The type was a green enamel vase on which was a relief of a princess sacrificing at an altar with some such inscription as "Good luck to Queen Berenice." These vases were bought as ornaments by loyal citizens and tourists. *Case G:* Funerary furniture; in the centre a skull, wreathed with artificial laurel. 3rd cent. B.C. (From the Chatby Necropolis, p. 178). *Case K:* Fine cinerary urns, dated—earliest, 281 B.C.—Right and left of the door into the gardens; Marble sarcophagi of the usual Alexandrian design. *Case P:* Glass vases of exquisite hue and design; there is more beauty in this little case than in tons of statues.

ROOM 18: Terra cotta Statuettes.

The statuettes, of which the best are Hellenistic and Alexandrian, were at first connected with funeral rites and later placed in the tomb from the sentiment that prompts us to drop flowers, especially when the dead person is young. They have mostly been found in the tombs of children and women. They are the loveliest things in the Museum.

Facing entrance, and to right (*Cases HH and A*): Cinerary urns from Alexandria.

Left wall: *Case F* (covered with curtain): Here are the masterpieces—27 statuettes of women. 1, 4, 7, 8, 12, 13, are the most beautiful perhaps—so delicate but so dignified. 1 is crowned with ivy and wears tiny earrings; the shape of her arm shown through the wrap that covers it. 7 carries her child. 12 with her little draped head is curiously impressive. *Case G:* 1. Child on his mother's shoulder. *Case H:* 1. Child on a toy chariot, full of grapes and drawn by dogs. *Case I:* Caricatures. *Case L:* Moulds for terra cotta. *Case* in corner, also *FF:* Fragments from Naucratis, the Greek predecessor of Alexandria in Egypt.

RIGHT WALL: Terra cottas from the Fayoum—stupid and vulgar.

DOWN THE CENTRE OF ROOM: Four mosaics from Canopus (p. 190); they probably decorated the Temple of Serapis there.

ROOM 19: MISCELLANEOUS.

IN ENTRANCE: Funerary urn still garlanded with artificial flowers. From Chatby. 3rd cent. B.C.

CENTRE: Mosaic—the best geometrical mosaic in the Museum. From Chatby.

IN ANGLES OF ROOM: *Cases A, B, C, D:* Terra cottas from Kom es Chogafa. Note in *Case C, Shelf b*, 1. Model of seven pots and a big jar—like doll's furniture; and in *Case D* some unamusing grotesques.

Also in the angles of the octagon: *Cases I, II, III, IV.* Funerary furniture from Hadra (p. 172). In *Case I* are two beautiful objects; a blue enamel vase decorated with faces of Bes, Egyptian god of luck; and (*Shelf b*, 2): Terra cotta statuette of a boy, who clings, laughing, to a term of Dionysus, and holds an apple in his hand.

ROOM 20: CHATBY NECROPOLIS (p. 178).

Several painted tombstones. The best are protected by tinted glass, and better studied in the water-colour copies hanging above.

LEFT OF ENTRANCE: 1. Isodora, a lady of Cyrene, with her child. 2. A young Macedonian officer, riding; his orderly runs behind holding the horse's tail. Date 4th cent. B.C.—*i.e.* shortly after Alexander had founded the city. 10231: Boy and child.

Cases A and *B:* Funerary furniture. In *Case B* are some pretty terra cottas: 1, 2. Ladies sitting. 7, 8, 9. Schoolgirls at lessons.

Pedestal V (right wall): Tombstone of young man with a foot-stool and pet dog.

CENTRE OF ROOM: Fine marble group, mutilated, of Dionysus and the Faun. Found near the demolished Porte Rosette.

ROOM 21: IBRAHIMIEH NECROPOLIS (p. 179).

Case in entrance: Wreaths of artificial flowers. Ugly really, but one is impressed by their being so old. Double flute of ivory.

Case in centre: Mummied birds from Aboukir (p. 188).

Cases D and *F:* From Ibrahimieh. *Case D.* Inscription in Aramaic—one of the few relics of the early Jewish settlement at Alexandria (p. 65); some more are on the floor. Date 3rd cent. B.C. *Case F* (right wall): Cinerary urns. Groups in painted plaster of the phallic Min (whom the Greeks identified with Pan), Hercules, Horus, etc.

ROOM 22: CANOPUS. (p. 190).

Disappointing; better work than this tenth rate Hellenistic stuff must have existed at the great shrine.

LEFT WALL: 1–3: Inscriptions of historical interest: they mention Serapis and Isis, the deities of the place, and the Ptolemies Philadelphus and Euergetes.

BACK WALL: In cases, sculptures and terra cottas.

RIGHT WALL: Stucco-coated columns from the Temple of Serapis; others have been left in place.

CENTRE: Mosaic from Alexandria.

ROOM 22A: FRESCOES.

RIGHT OF DOOR: Three pagan frescoes, connected with crocodile worship (*see* Room 7 and North Garden). From Temple of Petesouchos, Fayoum. Date 2nd cent. A.D. Thank offerings to the god from Heron Soubathos, an officer: 1. He stands. 2. He rides.

REST OF ROOM: Christian frescoes of great interest, from crypt discovered in the desert beyond Lake Mariout. Date 5th cent. A.D. A staircase led down to a square room. 1 and 2 are from the ceiling of this room; from its walls come— 3, St. Menas standing between camels—4 and 5, the Annunciation. A passage led to a smaller room; on its vault was 6, Head of Christ. In this smaller room were 7 and 8. Out of it opened a little niche at the end of which was 9, a saint in prayer among the scenery of paradise.

VERANDAH AND GARDENS. Large Exhibits.

In the middle of the verandah: Colossal headless statue of Hercules.

North Garden: Left—Gateways and shrine of the *Temple of Petesouchos,* crocodile god of the Fayoum (*see* Room 9 for further details). The first gateway is the entrance Pylon, over which is a Greek inscription dating the temple to B.C. 137. The wooden door in Room 9 belonged here. On each side of the gateway are lions. It led to a brick courtyard, in which was a Nilometer. The court was closed by the second gateway, which is flanked by sphinxes, and led to a second and similar court. Then comes the third gate, and, closing the perspective, the shrine. The shrine has three cavities, in each of which lurked a mummied crocodile upon a wooden stretcher (*see* Room 9). In the left cavity is the fresco of a crocodile; in the central the fresco of a god with a crocodile's head between two other deities. Over the cavities are several decorative friezes—one of snakes. The outside of the shrine is also frescoed to imitate marble. In front of it was found a wooden chest (Room 9).

At back of garden: Granite group of Rameses II and his daughter—headless. From Aboukir. Against the wall behind: colossal green granite head of Antony as Osiris. From near Nouzha (p. 172). The companion head of Cleopatra as Isis is in Belgium.

South garden: Two reconstructed tombs from the Chatby Necropolis (p. 178). The first (in the corner) is remarkable. The sarcophagus imitates a bed with cushions each end. The chamber where it stands was once preceded by a long vestibule for the mourners (as in the Anfouchi tombs, p. 137). The date 3rd. cent. B.C. The second tomb has a shell vault niche (like Kom es Chogafa, p. 163).

The Rue Rosette continues and at last issues from between houses. Here, ever since its foundation, the city has ended; in Ptolemaic times the Gate of the Sun or Canopic Gate stood here, in Arab times the Rosetta

Gate. The Public Gardens (left and right) follow the line of the Arab walls (see p. 86 and Section IV). The tramway to Nouzha crosses the route. The road continues under another name to Sidi Gaber (Section V), thence to Ramleh, and to Aboukir (Section VII). It is a good road and well planted; but terribly straight, like all roads that the Ancients have planned.

SECTION II

From the Square to Ras-el-Tin

ROUTE:—By the Rue de France and Rue Ras-el-Tin to Ras-el-Tin promontory; returning to the Square by Anfouchi Bay and the Eastern Harbour—the "Circular" Tram (Green Triangle) runs along the Quays.

CHIEF POINTS OF INTEREST:—Terbana and Chorbagi Mosques; Mosque of Abou-el-Abbas; Anfouchi Catacombs; Ras-el-Tin Palace; Prehistoric Harbour; Fort Kait Bey; New Quays.

We start from the northwest corner of the Square. The Rue de France traverses the "Turkish Town" (p. 90), which was built in the 17th and 18th cents. on the spit of land that had accreted round the ruined Ptolemaic dyke (p. 11). Its bazaars and Mosques are on a small scale, for the city was then at her feeblest. But the district is picturesque and, especially at evening, full of gentle charm. The best way of seeing it is to wander aimlessly about.

In the Rue de France:—Right: Rue Pirona. Built into the wall at its entrance are fragments of Egyptian sculpture, the lion-headed goddess Sekhet, &c. The road opens into a picturesque little square which contains a former Native Tribunal, and a building (No. 4) that has a carved gateway and a tranquil courtyard with antique columns.

In the roads to the left of the Rue de France are some Mosques:—

Mosque of Sheikh Ibrahim Pacha, off the southwest corner of the Square; big ugly building with red and yellow minaret.

Chorbagi Mosque, in the Rue el Midan. Well worth a visit. Date—1757. Plan—similar to the Terbana (*see* below). Exterior spoilt by restoration, but the door from the vestibule into the Mosque proper has over it a trefoil arch full of brilliant tiles; in the centre of the arch is a miniature praying niche (mihrab).—The Interior, though mean architecturally, retains its magnificent Tile Decoration almost intact. The tiles are grouped round the walls in great panels, the design being sometimes geometrical and sometimes a pot of flowers. Between the panels are bands of contrasting tiles. Colours:—in the panels, yellow, green, and a deep cornflower-blue predominate; in the bands, chinablue and white. A few of the panels are of polished conglomerate stone. The Prayer Niche—flanked by two bizarre twisted columns—has the pot of flowers design. The door of the pulpit is handsome; it has duplicated Cufic inscriptions, which on the right read from right to left, as is usual, and on the left are reversed for the sake of symmetry: a good instance of the decorative tendency of Arab Art. Externally the Mosque is flanked by arcades; one overlooks the street and is used by the Muezzin, since there is no minaret; the other looks into a courtyard of stilted arches.

Mosque of Abou Ali. (Go nearly to the end of the long Rue Bab-el-Akdar; thence, right, into Rue Masguid Ali Bey Guenenah; thence, right again). There is nothing to see in this humble little Mosque, but it is said to be the oldest in the city. In it are the figures 677, which, if they record the date A.H., would mean 1278 A.D. The natives say that it once stood at the edge of the sea, so that the faithful made their ablutions with salt water before praying. The tradition may be correct, for the old line of the coast lay here (*see* map p. 106). The building in its present appearance cannot be earlier than the 18th cent.; in it, perched on the summit of the pulpit, is the model of a boat.

Continuing from the Rue de France we see ahead the white mass of the *Terbana Mosque*.

Well worth visiting, in spite of modern plaster and paint. Date—1684. The little doorway on the street is in the "Delta" style—bricks painted black and red, with occasional courses of wood between them and Cufic inscriptions above: "There is no God but God," and "Mohammed is the Prophet of God"; better examples of the style at Rosetta (p. 199). The rest of the ground floor is occupied by shops. At the top of the stairs an interesting scene unfolds. To the left are two great antique granite columns with Corinthian capitals, and through them an open air terrace with an iron trellis and barred windows. To the right is the Vestibule of the Mosque, once very beautiful; two thirds of the entrance wall are still covered with tiles, designed like those in the Chorbagi, and over the door is the inscription "Built in 1097 A.H. by Haj Ibrahim Terbana," surmounted by a trefoil arch. More antique columns. The Interior is a rectangle, divided up by eight columns, disfigured but antique. Good painted ceiling, best seen from the western gallery. The Prayer Niche is finely tiled, as is the wall to its right; the large tiles with white daisies on them are inferior modern work. Lamentable chandeliers.—There is an external gallery with antique columns. The Minaret rises above the entrance landing; its topmost gallery is tiled.

The main route now takes the name Rue Ras-el-Tin. Here once began the southern shore of the Island of Pharos. Consequently ancient remains occur in situ.

Right: Rue Sidi Abou el Abbas leads to the square of that name—the most considerable in the Turkish Town; here, by evening light, one sometimes has the illusion of oriental romance; here (1922) is the rallying point of the Nationalist demonstrations. The road, just before it enters the square, crosses the site of a temple to Isis Pharia who watched over the lighthouse. (*see* coin in Museum, Room 2).

Dominating the square is the great white *Mosque of Abou el Abbas Moursi,* built 1767 by Algerians, some of whom still live in the neighbourhood; the tomb of the saint (d. 1288) is under a low dome; the other side of the Mosque (reached by a winding passage to the right) has an unrestored brick entrance in the "Delta" style, with pendentives, tiles, and a Cufic inscription.— At the end of the Square:—little *Mosque of Sidi Daoud,* with tomb of the saint, from whose precinct two tall palm trees rise.—Just off south side of square is a typical street tomb (Sidi Abou el Fath), enclosed in its green lattice; of the houses close to it No. 31 has good carved "Mashrabieh" work, No. 33 a carved lintel, with door posts of alternate courses of limestone and wood. All this tangle of lanes preserves the atmosphere of the 18th cent. East. Between the Abou el Abbas Mosque and the sea is a large modern Mosque—the Bouseiri— where the Sultan usually makes his Friday prayer; a little up the street is a stone fragment, covered with hieroglyphs, and now used upside down as a seat.

The Rue Ras-el-Tin is now joined by the "Circular" tram line. To the right is a large piece of waste ground. In the corner of this, close to the road, are some dilapidated glass roofs; these protect the Anfouchi Tombs; the custodian lives close by.

THE ANFOUCHI TOMBS

Though inferior to the Kom es Chogafa Catacombs, (p. 163), these tomb groups are interesting for their decoration scheme. Their entrances adjoin, their plan

I Vestibule
with scribblings

II Vestibule
with chessboard decorations

III Vestibule
with benches

IV Vestibule
with Roman additions

THE ANFOUCHI TOMBS

Right Hand
Group

Left Hand
Group

Hall

Hall

I

II

III.

IV

is similar:—a staircase, cut through the limestone, leads down to a square hall out of which the tomb chambers open. The decoration is of stucco painted to imitate marble blocks and tiles. It is shoddy, and sometimes recalls the imitation wall papers of Victorian England. Archaeologists know it as the First Pompeian style. Date:—Ptolemaic with Roman additions. Name of occupants: unknown.

RIGHT HAND TOMB GROUP (*see* Plan opposite).

At the first turn of the stairs, protected by a cloth, is a good picture. Subject:—Purification of the Dead by water (?); Horus, with a falcon's head, points with one hand to the land of death, and with the other tries to draw the dead man towards it; Osiris holds out a lustral vase; Isis is behind.—At the second turn of the stairs is another picture, half destroyed;—Osiris sits on a throne as king of the Dead with the dog-god Anubis behind him; before him, just discernible, stands Horus introducing the dead man.

Thus the staircase reminded visitors of the difficulties through which the dead must pass, and honoured Osiris, Isis, and their son Horus—a trinity whose worship was popular in Ptolemaic times and often connected with the worship of Serapis. The walls imitate alabaster &c.; on the vault, geometric designs.

The Hall is open to the air. It gives access to two tomb chambers, each of which has a vestibule for mourners. That to the right (i) is undecorated, but the scribblings on the vestibule walls are most amusing; they were made over 2,000 years ago by a visitor or workman, and help us to reconstruct the life of the Greco-Egyptian city. The inscriptions are in Greek. On the left wall Diodorus has immortalised Antiphiles, his friend. Further on is a sailing ship. Right wall, a battle ship with a turret for fighting, such as might have accompanied Cleopatra to Actium.

The vestibule in front (ii) is quite charming. It was decorated in the same style as the staircase—traces of this remains on the inside of its entrance wall—but soon after a fresh coat of stucco was applied, and painted like the first to imitate marble, but in better taste. Below, is a dado of "alabaster," above it an effective design of black and white squares arranged chess board fashion and divided by alabaster bands. In the chess board are mythological scenes, now defaced. The ceiling, being purely geometric, probably belongs to the earlier scheme.

At the end of the vestibule is the entrance to the tomb chamber, with the disc of the Sun (Ra) carved above it, and, on either side, little sleeping sphinxes upon pedestals. A door once closed it; holes for the bolt remain. The tomb chamber itself is decorated in the same pretty style. An altar once stood in the middle. In the back wall is a tiny shrine, closing the vista. The general effect is good, but dainty rather than solemn; the terrors of ancient Egypt are on the wane.

LEFT HAND TOMB GROUP.

The vestibule in front, as one enters the Hall, is very long, and low benches on which the mourners sat run up it on each side. (iii). In the tomb chamber is an enormous sarcophagus of rose coloured granite from Assouan.

The vestibule and tomb chamber to the left (iv) were excavated and decorated on the usual plan. But in the Roman period they were much pulled about, and brick work introduced, together with three new sarcophagi.

There are traces of other tombs over the waste ground, which covers the cemetery of the ancient Island of Pharos. We are now in the centre of the Island, and about to visit its western extremity.

Straight ahead, up a rise, is *Ras-el-Tin Palace*, the summer residence of the Sultan, who makes his state entry every June. It was built by Mohammed Ali (p. 94), who had here the stormy interview with Sir Charles Napier, that ended his loftier ambitions (p. 95); Ismail restored it; Tewfik was here during some of the troubles of 1882 (p. 101). It is not ugly, as palaces go; the grandiose classical portico is rather impressive. To the right are the barracks.

The peninsula narrows. The road leads on to the Yacht Club (left), and terminates at the Military Hospital which is beautifully situated on the rocky point of Ras-el-Tin (the "Cape of Figs"); splendid views of the Western Harbour and the sea; a Temple of Neptune once stood here, and there are ruins of tombs all along the northern shore. A modern lighthouse stands in the Hospital enclosure, and marks the entrance to the harbour. The Breakwater (constructed 1870–74) starts below, makes towards the isolated rock of Abou Bakr, then bends to the left. Over the water are the island of Marabout and the headland of Agame, which are part of the same limestone chain as Ras-el-Tin, and connected with it by submarine reefs.

The sea west and north of the point is full of remains of the Prehistoric Harbour.

PREHISTORIC HARBOUR

For details of this important and mysterious work see "Les Ports submergés de l'ancienne Isle de Pharos" by M. Jondet, the discoverer. Possibly it may be the harbour alluded to in the Odyssey (*see* p. 6), but no historian mentions it. Theosophists, with more zeal than probability, have annexed it to the vanished civilisation of Atlantis; M. Jondet inclines to the theory that it may be Minoan—built by the maritime power of Crete. If Egyptian in origin, perhaps the work of Rameses II (B.C. 1300); statues of his reign have been found on Rhakotis (p. 7), and we know that he was attacked by "peoples of the West," and built defences against them. It cannot be as late as Alexander the Great or we should have records. It is the oldest work in the district and also the most romantic, for to its antiquity is added the mystery of the sea.

Long and narrow, the Harbour stretched from the rock

of Abou Bakr on the west to an eastern barrier that touched the shore beyond the Tour de la Mission d'Egypt. These two points are joined up by a series of breakwaters on the north. The entrance was from an unexpected direction, the south. Having rounded Abou Bakr, ships turned north under the Ras-el-Tin promontory, where there is deep water. To their left were solid quays, stretching to Abou Bakr, and recently utilised in the foundation of the modern breakwater. To their right was another quay. Having entered, they were well in the middle of the main harbour, with a subsidiary harbour to the north.

The visit to the Harbour is best made by boat, since most of the remains now lie from 4 to 25 feet under the sea. They have, like all the coast line, subsided, because the Nile deposits on which they stand are apt to compress, and even to slide towards deeper water. They are built of limestone blocks from the quarries of Mex and Dekhela, but the construction, necessarily simple, gives no hint as to nationality or date. The modern breakwater, being built across the entrance, makes the scheme rather difficult to follow. (*See* Plan).

The Small Quay (*a*) is in perfect condition, and not four feet under water. Length: 70 yards, breadth, 15; the surface curves slightly towards the south. The blocks, measuring about a yard each, are cut to fit one another roughly, small stones filling up the joints. The Ras-el-Tin jetty crosses the end of this Quay; the point of intersection is near the red hut on the jetty.—At the north end of the Quay is an extension (*b*) that protected the harbour entrance.

Further north, well inside the harbour, is an islet (*c*) covered with remains. Some are tombs, and of later date; submerged, are the foundations of a rectangular building (30 yds. by 15) reached on the south by steps, and connected by little channels with the sea on the

THE PREHISTORIC HARBOUR

Modern work shown thus ....
Ancient work shown thus ━━━━━

RAS EL TIN

Eastern Barrier

Ancient Breakwaters

h

g

Outer Harbour

i

g

g

MAIN HARBOUR

Quays

d

Rock of Abu Bakr

e

f

Breakwater

Main Entrance (Modern)

Military Hospital

Quay

a

b

c

MODERN HARBOUR

north. This islet may have contained the harbour offices.

From the modern breakwater the Great Quays (*d*) show here and there as ochreous lines below the waves. They are 700 yds. long, and constructed like the Small Quay, but from larger stones. They connect with the rock of Abou Bakr (*e*), the western bastion of the Pre-historic Harbour; it is a solid mass over 200 yds. square; most is on the sea level, but a part juts up; it is marked all over with foundation cuts and the remains of ma-sonry. West of Abou Bakr is a double breakwater (*f*) further protecting the works from the sea and the prev-alent wind; and on it hinges the huge northern break-water (*g*) also double in parts, which runs with inter-ruptions till it reaches the eastern barrier (*h*). The rock is named after the first Caliph of Islam.

The outer harbour (*i*) has not yet been fully ex-plored.

Having returned as far as Ras-el-Tin Palace, we bear to the left, and follow the tram line along the shore of Anfouchi Bay. The Bay is very shallow and the en-trance is protected by reefs. Pirates used it once. Na-tive boat builders work along its beach and are pleas-ant to watch. In the corner is Anfouchi Pier, with a bathing establishment; beyond, on a small promontory, stands all that is left of Fort Adda; Arabi had his pow-der stored here in 1882, and the English blew it up (p. 100). Now the tram turns a sharp corner, and a sec-ond Fort swings into view—Fort Kait Bey.

FORT KAIT BEY (THE "PHAROS")

This battered and neglected little peninsula is per-haps the most interesting spot in Alexandria, for here,

rising to an incredible height, once stood the Pharos
Lighthouse, the wonder of the world. Contrary to general belief, some fragments of the Pharos still remain.
But before visiting them and the Arab fort in which
they are imbedded, some knowledge of history is desirable. The fortunes of the peninsula were complicated, and the labours of scholars have only lately
made them clear.

HISTORY.

(1) THE ORIGINAL BUILDING (*see* also p. 17).

The lighthouse took its name from Pharos Island (hence
the French "phare" and the Italian "faro"). No doubt it
entered into Alexander the Great's scheme for his maritime
capital, but the work was not done till the reign of Ptolemy
Philadelphus. Probable date of dedication: B.C. 279, when
the king held a festival to commemorate his parents. Architect: Sostratus, an Asiatic Greek. The sensation it
caused was tremendous. It appealed both to the sense of
beauty and to the taste for science—an appeal typical of
the age. Poets and engineers combined to praise it. Just as
the Parthenon had been identified with Athens and St.
Peter's was to be identified with Rome, so, to the imagination of contemporaries, the Pharos became Alexandria and
Alexandria became the Pharos. Never, in the history of architecture, has a secular building been thus worshipped
and taken on a spiritual life of its own. It beaconed to the
imagination, not only to ships at sea, and long after its
light was extinguished memories of it glowed in the minds
of men.

It stood in a colonnaded court. (Plan II, p. 149.) There
were four stories. (Plan I, Fig. i.) The square bottom storey
was pierced with many windows and contained the rooms,
estimated at 300, where the mechanics and attendants were
housed. There was a spiral ascent—probably a double spiral
—and in the centre there may have been hydraulic machinery for raising fuel to the top; otherwise we must imagine
a procession of donkeys who cease not night and day to go
up and down the spirals with loads of wood on their backs.

The storey ended in a square platform and a cornice and figures of Tritons. Here too, in great letters of lead, was the Greek inscription; "Sostratus of Cnidos, son of Dexiphanes: to the Saviour Gods: for sailors"—an inscription which, despite its simplicity, bore a double meaning. The "Saviour Gods" are of course Castor and Pollux who protect mariners, but a courtly observer could refer them to Ptolemy Soter and Berenice, whose worship their son was promoting.

The second storey was octagonal and entirely filled by the spiral ascent. Above that was the circular third storey, and above that the lantern. The lighting arrangements are uncertain. Visitors speak of a mysterious "mirror" on the summit, which was even more wonderful than the building itself. What was this "mirror"? Was it a polished steel reflector for the fire at night or for heliography by day? Some accounts describe it as made of finely wrought glass or transparent stone, and declare that a man sitting under it could see ships at sea that were invisible to the naked eye. A telescope? Is it possible that the great Alexandrian school of mathematics discovered the lens, and that their discovery was lost and forgotten when the Pharos fell? It is possible. It is certain that the lighthouse was fitted with every scientific improvement known to the age, that the antique world never surpassed it, and that the mediaeval world regarded it as the work of Jinns.

Standing on the lantern was a statue of Poseidon. This terminated the tower, whose complete height certainly exceeded 400 feet and possibly touched 500.

(2) HISTORY OF THE BUILDING.

We must now follow this masterpiece of engineering into ages of myth and oblivion. It retained its form and functions unimpaired up to the Arab Conquest (A.D. 641). The first, and irreparable, disaster was the fall of the lantern (about 700), entailing the loss of scientific apparatus that could not be replaced. There is a legend that the disaster was planned by the Byzantine Emperor, who could not attack Egypt owing to the magic "mirror," which detected or destroyed his ships. He sent an agent who gained the

Caliph's confidence and told him that beneath the Pharos the treasure of Alexander the Great lay buried. The Caliph commenced demolition, and before the inhabitants of Alexandria, who knew better, could intervene, the two upper stories had fallen into the sea. Henceforth the Pharos is only a stump with a bonfire on the top.

There were restorations under Ibn Touloun (880), and also about 980, but they were unsubstantial additions to the Octagon, which the wind could blow away. Structural repairs were neglected, and about 1100 the second disaster occurred—the fall of the Octagon itself through an earthquake. The square bottom storey survived, but only as a watchtower on the top of which was run up a small square Mosque. (See Plan I, Fig. ii, which illustrates this state of the Pharos. The level of the ground has risen owing to the debris from the octagon, and the lower storey has been buttressed.) Then came the final earthquake (14th cent.), and the slow dissolution was over.

Though unable to preserve the Pharos the Arabs admired it, and speak, with their love of the marvellous, of a statue on it whose finger followed the diurnal course of the sun, of a second statue who gave out with varying and melodious voices the various hours of the day, and of a third who shouted an alarm as soon as a hostile flotilla set sail. The first two statues may have existed; the Alexandrians loved such toys. And there is an element of truth in another Arab legend—that the building rested upon a "glass crab." Some vitreous composition probably did form the foundation, and we know that "Cleopatra's Needles" actually did rest on crabs of metal (p. 176); the oriental mind has confused the two monuments. The legend culminates in the visit to the Pharos of a cavalcade of horsemen who lose their way in the 300 rooms, and inadvertently riding into a crack in the glass crab's back fall into the sea! But sometimes the lighthouse sheltered pleasanter adventures. The poet El Deraoui, for example, writes:

A lofty platform guides the voyager by night, guides him with its light when the darkness of evening falls.

Tritons **Tritons**

Greek
Inscription

Fig. I
The Pharos as built
by Sostratus

Fig. II
The Pharos in the
Arab Period

Fig. III
The Castle before
1882

KAIT BEY PLAN I

KAIT BEY PLAN II

Thither have I borne a garment of perfect pleasure among my friends, a garment adorned with the memory of beloved companions.

On its height a dome enshadowed me, and thence I saw my friends like stars.

I thought that the sea below me was a cloud, and that I had set up my tent in the midst of the heavens.

Moreover "El Manarah," as the Arabs called it, gave the name to, and became the model for, the "minaret." There is no minaret in Alexandria that closely follows the Pharos, but at Cairo (*e.g.* at the Tombs of the Mamelukes) one can still see the square bottom storey, the Octagon, the Round and the Summit that exactly reproduce the four-stage design of Sostratus.

(3) FORT KAIT BEY.

For a hundred years ruins cumbered the peninsula. Then (1480) the Mameluke Sultan Kait Bey fortified it as part of his coast defence against the Turks, who had taken Constantinople and were threatening Egypt (p. 87). Kait Bey is a great figure at Cairo, where mosques commemorate his glorious reign. Here he only builds a fort, but like all his work it is architecturally fine, and even in decay its outlines are harmonious. The scheme was a pentagon (Plan II) and in the enclosed area, on the exact site of the Pharos, stood a square castle or keep with a mosque embedded in it. (Plan I, Fig. iii, which shows the castle before it was ruined, the minaret sticking up inside it.) The Turks effected their conquest in 1517, and when their power in its turn declined, Mohammed Ali (1805–1848) modernised the defences. No visitors were admitted, and the Fort gained the reputation of an impregnable and mysterious place. Its career ended with the English bombardment of 1882. Though it did not suffer as much as its neighbour Fort Adda, damage enough was done. The castle was shattered, the minaret snapped, and the desolation and squalor re-established that brood there to-day.

We can now examine the existing remains. (*See* Plans I & II pp. 148, 149.)

The connecting spit of land only formed in the 9th cent. Previously there was shallow water, spanned by a bridge. Right, as we approach, is anchorage for an Italian fishing fleet; the men come from Bari in the Adriatic.—The road leads by the side of the fort to the new breakwater, built to protect the Eastern Harbour and the sea wall. The Breakwater is a noble work, and it is a pity it is approached through a gateway that suggests an English provincial Jail; the embellishments of modern Alexandria are unduly lugubrious.

The blocked up *Gateway* to the Fort is flanked by round towers; inside it are several rooms with 15th cent. vaulting.—To its left, built into the masonry of Kait Bey's wall or lying on the beach, are about thirty *broken columns* of red Assouan granite; also two or three pieces of fine speckled granite and one piece of marble. These are survivals from the Pharos, and may have stood in the colonnade of its surrounding court; the sea wall of that court probably diverged here from the line of Kait Bey's wall; there are traces of cutting among the rocks.

The interior of the Fort (best entered from the right) is now a bare enclosure with a few coast-guard huts. The isolated lump of building at the end is the remains of Kait Bey's *Castle,* occupying the ground plan of the Pharos and utilising in part its foundations. Some of these foundations can be seen in the passage immediately to the right of the Castle. The orientation of the Castle and the Pharos was not exactly the same, since the Castle had to be adjusted to the points of the compass on account of the mosque that it contained.— The modern buildings to the right of the passage also rest on old foundations; it is thought that here stood the reservoir, filled with fresh water from the mainland and that on the other side (left of present Castle) stood another edifice with the mechanical statues to balance the design. But this is all conjecture.

The *Mosque* in the Castle is notable for two reasons: architecturally it is the oldest in the city, and in style it is essentially Cairene. It was built by the central government in the course of their coast defence scheme, and so does not resemble the ordinary mosque of the Delta. The entrance, with its five monoliths of Assouan granite, taken from the Pharos, is almost druidical in effect, but the arch above them and the flanking towers faintly recall the glories of Kait Bey's work at Cairo. In the vestibule are remains of stucco on the ceiling and marble on the floor.—The actual Mosque is of the "school" type—a square with an arched recess opening out of each side, each recess being assigned to one of the four orthodox sects of Islam; the Mosque of Sultan Hassan at Cairo is a famous example of this type. The square, and the step leading up to each recess are inlaid with marble. Light enters through carved woodwork above.

Over the Mosque are vaulted rooms. From the summit of the mass is a *View* of Alexandria, not beautiful but instructive. From right to left are:—Fort Adda, Ras-el-Tin lighthouse (background); minarets of Abou el Abbas and Bouseiri Mosques (foreground); Kom-el-Nadur Fort; Terbana Mosque (foreground); "Pompey's Pillar" (back); Kom-el-Dik Fort; the long line of Eastern suburbs; beyond them the distant minaret of Sidi Bishr; the coast ends in the wooded promontory of Montazah. Close beneath is the modern Breakwater stretching towards the opposing promontory of Silsileh; and left, awash with waves, the Diamond Rock.—And now let the visitor (if the effort is not beyond him) elevate himself 400 feet higher into the air. Let him replace the Ras-el-Tin lighthouse by a Temple to Poseidon; let him delete the mosques and the ground they stand on, and imagine in their place an expanse of water crossed by a Dyke; let him add to "Pompey's Pillar" the Temple of Serapis and Isis and the vast buttressed walls of the Library; let him turn Kom-el-Dik into a gorgeous and fantastic park, with the Tomb of Alexander at its feet; and the Eastern suburbs into gardens; and finally let him suppose that it is not Silsileh that stretches towards him but the peak of the Ptolemaic Palace, sheltering to its right the ships of the royal fleet and flanked on the landward side by the tiers of the theatre and the groves of the Mouseion.— Then he may have some conception of what Ancient Alexandria looked like from the summit of the Pharos —what she looked like when the Arabs entered in the autumn of 641.

Beneath the Batteries on the north of the Fort, and almost level with the beach, is a long gallery in which lie some shells that were fired by the English in 1882.

The tram now follows the curve of the *Eastern Harbour*, a beautifully shaped basin. It was the main harbour of the ancients, but Mohammed Ali when he planned the modern city, developed the Western instead (p. 97). There is a sea wall in two stages, to break the waves which dash right on to the road in rough weather; and there is a very fine promenade—the New Quays—which stretches all the way from Kait Bey to Silsileh. A walk along it can be delightful, though occasionally marred by bad smells.—We pass, right, the Bouseiri Mosque (*see* above) and finally come to the French Gardens, that connect with the Square, whence we started.

Left of the French Gardens are: the French Consulate—an isolated building; the General Post Office—entered from the road behind; and the Church of St. Andrew's—Church of Scotland. To the right, down Rue de l'Eglise Maronite, is the Maronite Church, an inoffensive building; (for the Maronites *see* pp. 82, 229).

SECTION III

From the Square to
the Southern Quarters

ROUTE:—By the Place St. Catherine and "Pompey's Pillar" to the Mahmoudieh Canal, taking the Karmous Tram (Green Lozenge). The Ragheb Pasha Tram (Red Crescent) and the Moharrem Bey Tram (Red Circle) also go from the Square to the Canal. There is also the "Circular" Tram (Green Triangle) which crosses the three lines just mentioned, on its course from Cairo Railway Station to the Docks. There is a carriage road along the Canal.

CHIEF POINTS OF INTEREST:—"Pompey's Pillar," Kom-es-Chogafa Catacombs, the Canal.

The Southern Quarters are neither smart nor picturesque. But they include the site of Rhakotis, the nucleus of ancient Alexandria, and preserve some remarkable antiquities (*see* pp. 7, 21). Here too are the churches and schools of the various religious and political bodies (*see* p. 227).

We start from the south side of the Square, and immediately reach the *Place St. Catherine*, a triangular green. Here is the traditional site of St. Catherine's martyrdom, whence she was transported to Mount Sinai by angels. But the legend only dates from the 9th cent. and it is unlikely that the saint ever existed (*see* p. 51). Franciscans settled here in the 15th cent. and built a church that has disappeared. In 1832 Mo-

hammed Ali granted land to the Roman Catholics, and
the present *Cathedral Church of St. Catherine* was begun. It fell down while it was being put up, but un-
deterred by the omen the builders persisted, and here
is the result. Gaunt without and tawdry within, the
Cathedral makes no attempt to commemorate the exquisite legend round which so much that is beautiful
has gathered in the West; St. Catherine of Alexandria
is without grace in her own city. The approach to the
church has however a certain ecclesiastic calm.—Behind (entered from Rue Sidi el Metwalli) is the Catholic Archbishop's Palace; the wayside tomb of the Mohammedan Saint Sidi el Metwalli, a prior arrival, abuts
into his Grace's garden.

Left of the Cathedral is another in equally bad taste
—the Cathedral of the Greek Community (Greek Orthodox) dedicated to the Annunciation. The Schools of
the Community are close to it.

Left, after leaving the Place St. Catherine:—Rue Sidi
el Metwalli, following the line of the ancient Canopic
Way; it leads past the *Attarine Mosque,* which is worth
looking at. In the past, buildings of greater importance
stood on this commanding site. Here was a church to
St. Athanasius, dedicated soon after his death (4th
cent.). In the Arab Conquest (7th cent.) the church
was adapted into a great mosque, square in shape like
the Mosque of Ibn Touloun at Cairo, and stretching
some way to the north of the present building; travellers mistook it for the tomb or the palace of Alexander
the Great. In it stood an ancient sarcophagus, weighing
nearly seven tons. The English, informed that Alexander had once lain here, took the sarcophagus away
when they occupied Alexandria in 1801 (*see* p. 93).
The French protested, and the sheikhs of the Mosque,
deeply moved, came down to the boat to bid the relic
farewell. The sarcophagus is now in the British Mu-

seum, and has proved to belong to the native Pharaoh Nekht Heru Hebt, B.C. 378.—The present Mosque is wedge shaped with a minaret at the point; a good little specimen of modern Mohammedan architecture. It has a second façade in the Rue Attarine, (Scent Bazaar) whence its name. Inside is the Tomb of Said Mohammed (13th cent.), a friend of Abou el Abbas (p. 137). —Beyond it the road becomes the Rue Rosette (*see* Section I); right is the American Mission Church and the Cairo Station.

Right after leaving the Place:—district inhabited by the Armenian community (*see* p. 229). Their church is simple and rather attractive, and has the projecting western vestibule characteristic of Armenian architecture, *e.g.* of the Metropolitan Cathedral of Etchmiadzine. In the graveyard are monuments of Nubar Pasha by Puech (*see* p. 170), and of Takvor Pasha. In the grounds of the school, a black basalt sphinx.

Straight ahead after leaving the Place: is the Rue Abou el Dardaa. In a turning out of it to the right (Rue Prince Moneim) in the grounds of a florist named Mousny, are some remains of the *Old Protestant Cemetery.*—The burials are of a later date than those at St. Saba (p. 114). The most interesting is the Tomb of Henry Salt. Salt, a vigorous but rather shady Englishman with an artistic temperament, first came to these parts in 1809, when he was sent on a mission to Abyssinia. Six years later he became Consul General and fell in with the financial plans of Mohammed Ali (p. 95) and acquiesced in his illegal monopolies. He was an ardent archaeologist of the commercial type and got concessions for excavating in Upper Egypt, offering the results, at exorbitant rates, to the British Museum. After much haggling the Museum bought his collection in 1823. He died near Alexandria in 1827. The quaint inscription on his tomb says:—

His ready genius explored and elucidated the Hiero-
glypics (sic) and other antiquities of this country. His
faithful and rapid pencil and the nervous originality of
his untutored senses conveyed to the world vivid ideas
of the scenes that had delighted himself.

Some of the tombs are hidden among plants and ferns.
The Cemetery was once much larger; the road has cut
through it.

At the end of the Rue Abou el Dardaa, where the
tram turns, is the *Mosque of Amr*. Here probably stood
the Mosque of Mercy which the conqueror Amr ordered to be built where he had sheathed his sword
after the recapture of the city in 643 (*see* p. 62).

We turn right for a few yards, along a road that follows the line of the vanished Arab Walls (p. 86). Then
to the left by the big Italian schools. The tram has now
entered the ancient district of Rhakotis.

"POMPEY'S PILLAR" and the TEMPLE
OF SERAPIS

As often happens in Alexandria, history and archaeology fail to support one another. Ancient writers do
not mention "Pompey's Pillar," but they tell us a great
deal about the buildings that stood in its neighbourhood and have now disappeared. This shapeless hill
was from early times covered with temples and houses.
Long before Alexander came it was the citadel of
Rhakotis (p. 7). Osiris was worshipped here. Then
with Ptolemy Soter it leaps into fame. Osiris is modified
into Serapis (p. 20), and the hill, encased in great bas-
tions of masonry was built up into an acropolis on
whose summit rose the God's temple. Under Cleopatra
it gained additional splendour. The great Library of

Mohammedan

Remains of
Temple of Isis

Fragments
of columns

Remains
of Temple of
Serapis

N
W — E
S

Scale: $\frac{1}{1.000}$

POMPEY'S PILLAR, ETC.

Cemetery

To Alexandria

To Kôm esch Chogafa Catacombs

Tram

Granite
Fragments

Entrance

Pompey's
Pillar

Sphinxes

Substructures

Remains

Remains

Alexandria had been burnt in the Caesarian war, and the queen began a new collection which she attached to the Serapeum. Here for four hundred years was the most learned spot on the earth. The Christians wiped it out. In 391 the Patriarch Theophilus (p. 55) led a mob against the temple, sacked it, and broke the statue of the God. It is impossible that the books should not have perished at the same time: they were arranged in the cloisters that surrounded the temple (*see* below) so that the mob had to pass them to reach its central prey. The monks now swarmed over the hill and built a church to St. John the Baptist in the gutted shrine. Here were the headquarters of Theophilus' nephew, Cyril (p. 56) and hence his supporters issued to murder Hypatia at the other end of the town (415). With the invasion of the Arabs the darkness increases. The Library had already disappeared (the legend accusing them of burning it has the flimsiest foundations), but they did plenty of harm in other ways: one of the Arab governors threw a quantity of columns into the sea in the hope of obstructing a hostile fleet. When the Crusaders visited Egypt (15th cent.) the original scheme of the Acropolis had vanished, and their attention was caught by this solitary pillar. The Crusaders were no scholars but they had heard of Pompey, so they called the pillar after him, and said that his head was enclosed in a ball on the top (*see* Belon's View p. 89). The error has been perpetuated and the visitor must remember, firstly that the pillar has nothing to do with Pompey and secondly that it is a subordinate monument that the accident of time has preserved: it is a part and a small one of the splendours of the Temple of Serapis.

The following remains can be visited (*see* Plan p. 158).

(i). *"Pompey's Pillar."* 84 feet high and about 7

thick; made of red granite from Assouan. An imposing but ungraceful object. Architecture has evolved nothing more absurd than the monumental column; there is no reason that it should ever stop nor much that it should begin, and this specimen is not even well proportioned. The substructure is interesting. It is made up of blocks that have been taken from older buildings. On the eastern face (nearest turnstile) is a block of green granite with an inscription in Greek in honour of Arsinoe, the sister and wife of Ptolemy Philadelphus (p. 16). On the opposite face (upside down in a recess) is the figure and hieroglyph of Seti I (B.C. 1350), suggesting the great age of the settlement on Rhakotis.

Why and when was the pillar put up?

Probably to the Emperor Diocletian, about A.D. 297. There is a four line Greek inscription to him on the granite base on the western side, about 10 feet up. It is illegible and indeed invisible from the ground. Generations of scholars have worked at it with the following result:—

"To the most just Emperor, the tutelary God of Alexandria, Diocletian the invincible: Postumus, prefect of Egypt."

The formidable Emperor (p. 51) had crushed a rebellion here and was a god to be propitiated; the Pillar, erected in the precincts of Serapis, would celebrate his power and clemency and presumably bore his statue on the top.—There is another theory: that the column was dedicated after the triumph of the Christians in 391 and glorifies the new religion; if this is so it must itself have previously been pagan, for by this date the Alexandrians had not the means or the power to erect a new monument of such a size.

(ii). *The Temple of Serapis.* West of the Pillar, reached by a staircase, are long subterranean galleries,

excavated in the rock and lined with limestone. These
were probably part of the Serapeum—basements of
some sort—and enthusiastic visitors have even identified them with the library where the books were kept;
in them are some small semicircular niches of unknown
use. Some marble columns stand on the ground above.
—South of the Pillar, near the Sphinxes, are more passages, lined with cement; these too may have been part
of the temple. All is conjectural, and the plan of the
Serapeum, as we gather it from classical writers, can
in no way be fitted in with existing remains. According
to them, it was rectangular, and stood in the middle of
a cloister, with each of whose sides it was connected
by a cross-colonnade. The temple consisted of a great
hall and an inner shrine. The architecture was probably Greek; certainly the statue was—made of blue-
black marble (p. 21), the work of Bryaxis.

(iii). *The Temple of Isis.* Isis, wife of Osiris, was
equally united to his successor Serapis, and had in
Ptolemaic times her temple on the plateau. North of
the Pillar are some excavations that have been identified with it.

(iv). *Two Sphinxes.* Found in the enclosure and set
up south of the Pillar. Of Assouan granite.

(v). *Fragments of a Frieze.* These, magnificently
worked in granite, lie on the slope east of the Pillar;
we pass them on the way up. Date:—about 1st cent.
A.D. They may have belonged to the great entrance
gate of the temple enclosure. He who meditates on
them for a little may recapture some idea of the shrine.
Not the Pillar itself so suggests vanished glory and
solidity.

This concludes the remains. They are disappointing
for so famous a site, but there is one satisfaction: this
is the actual spot. Long in doubt, it has been identified
by the statues and inscriptions that have been found

here; they are now in the Museum (*see* Rooms 6, 12, and 16).

Just beyond the enclosure of "Pompey's Pillar" we leave the tram route and turn to the right, reaching in ten minutes the Kom es Chogafa Catacombs.

CATACOMBS OF KOM ES CHOGAFA

Through the turnstile (5 piastres) is modern asphalt laid down to preserve the subterraneans from wet. Left, four fine sarcophagi of purplish granite. Above, the original level of the hill, which has been cut down by quarrying and excavations; in its slopes are some cemented passages, antique but uninteresting. On the top of the hill, a mosaic of black and white stones, much broken away. The entrance to the catacombs is down the larger of the two glassed well-shafts.

The Catacombs of Kom es Chogafa ("Hill of Tiles") are the most important in the city and unique anywhere: nothing quite like them has been discovered. They are unique both for their plan and for their decorations which so curiously blend classical and Egyptian designs; only in Alexandria could such a blend occur. Their size, their picturesque vistas, their eerie sculptures, are most impressive, especially on a first visit. Afterwards their spell fades for they are odd rather than beautiful, and they express religiosity rather than religion. Date—about the 2nd cent. A.D. when the old faiths began to merge and melt. Name of occupants—unknown. There is a theory that they began as a family vault which was developed by a burial syndicate. They were only discovered in 1900.

The scheme should be grasped before descending;

KOM ES CHOGAFA
PLAN OF CHIEF CHAMBERS

First Story ----------
Second Story ————

A	Well Staircase
B	Vestibule
C	Rotunda
D	Banquet Hall
E	Staircase
F	Vestibule
G I II III	Central Tomb
H	Passage
I	Tomb Chamber
J	Gallery
K	Square Well
L	Hall of Caracalla
M	Gallery of Painted Tomb

there are three stories, the lowest is under water. (*See* Plan opposite.)

The Staircase (A) is lit from a well, down which the dead bodies were lowered by ropes.—It ends at the Vestibule (B). Here are two semicircular niches, each fitted with a bench and elegantly vaulted with a shell—a classical motive unknown to the art of ancient Egypt. Close by is the Rotunda (C): in its centre is a well, upon whose parapet stand 8 pillars, supporting a domed roof. A circular passage runs round the well.—Left from the Rotunda is the Banquet Hall (D), where the friends and relatives ate ceremonially in memory of the dead. It is a gloomy scene. Here, cut out of the limestone, are the three couches where they reclined upon mattresses; the table in the middle has disappeared; it was probably of wood. Pillars support the roof.—From the Rotunda a Staircase (E) goes down to the second storey; the amazing Central Tomb is now revealed; weird effects can be got by adjusting the electric lights. The Staircase is roofed by a shell ornament; half-way down, it divides on each side a thing that looks like a prompter's box; this masks yet another staircase that descends to the third storey, now under water.

THE CENTRAL TOMB.

In the Vestibule (F) the Egyptian note predominates. In front, two fine columns with ornate capitals and two pilasters with square papyrus capitals—the four supporting a cornice adorned with the winged Sun (Ra), and guardian falcons. Inside the Vestibule, to right and left, are white limestone statues of a man and woman—the proprietor and his wife, perhaps. On the further wall the religious and artistic confusion increases. Two terrific bearded serpents guard the entrance to the Tomb Chamber, and each not only enfolds the pine-cone of Dionysus and the serpent-wand of Hermes, but also wears the double crown of Upper and Lower Egypt. Above each serpent is a Medusa in a round shield. Over the lintel of the inner door is the winged Sun and a frieze of snakes.

The Tomb Chamber (G) contains three large sarcophagi, all cut out of the rock. They are classical in style—decorated with festoons of fruit or flowers, Medusa heads, Ox skulls, &c. The lids do not take off; the mummies would have been pushed in from the passage behind (*see* below). But as a matter of fact none of the three sarcophagi have ever been occupied; it is part of the queerness of Kom-es-Chogafa that its vast and elaborate apparatus for mourning should culminate in a void.

In the niche over each sarcophagus are bas reliefs, Egyptian in style but executed with imperfect understanding.

Centre niche (G.i). A mummy on a lion shaped bier: the lion wears the crown of Osiris and has at its feet the feather of Maat, goddess of truth. Behind the bier, Anubis as the god of embalming; at its head Thoth with the symbol of immortality; at its foot, Horus; beneath it three "Canopic" deities—vases for the intestines—there ought to be four. —Lateral relief: Left, a man with a priest, right, a woman with a priest.

Right hand niche (G.ii). Graceful design of a prince, who wears the double crown of Egypt, offering a collar to the Apis Bull, who, with the Sun between his horns stands on a pedestal. Behind Apis, Isis, holding the feather of truth and stretching out her protective wings with good decorative effect.—Lateral reliefs: Left, a king before a god (Chons ?); right, two "Canopic" deities, one ape headed, one a mummy.

Left hand niche (G.iii). Similar to right hand, except that on the right lateral wall one of the "Canopic" deities has the head of a hawk.

On either side of the entrance door stands an uncanny figure. Right, (as one goes out) is Anubis, with a dog's head, but dressed up as a Roman soldier, with cuirass, short sword, lance and shield complete. Left, the god Sebek, who though mainly a crocodile is also crushed into military costume with cloak and spear. Perhaps the queer couple were meant to guard the tomb, but one must not read too much into them or into anything here; the workmen employed were only concerned to turn out a room that should look suitable for death, and judged by this standard they have succeeded.

Surrounding the central tomb is a broad Passage (HHH) lined with cavities in two rows that provided accommodation for nearly 300 mummies. Where the passage passes behind the central tomb one can see the apertures through which the three grand sarcophagi were hollowed out, and through which the mummies would have been introduced. Leading out of this passage is another tomb-chamber (I) and, to the left, a big Gallery (JJJJ), fitted up with receptacles in the usual style.

All the above chambers form part of a single scheme. We now return to the Rotunda (C), and enter, through a breach in the rock, an entirely distinct set of tombs. They are lighted by a square Well (K) and were reached by a separate staircase now ruinous. The Hall (L) is fancifully called the Hall of Caracalla because that emperor massacred many Alexandrian youths whom he had summoned to a review, and because many bones of men and horses have been found intermingled on its floors; it is lined with tomb cavities on the usual plan.—The Gallery (M) contains rather a charming tomb: it was once covered with white stucco and delicately painted. In the niche above the sarcophagus are Isis and her sister Nephtys, spreading their wings over the mummy of Osiris. More figures on the lateral walls. Above, on the inner wall, the soul as a bird. Above the entrance, the Sun and golden Vase on either side of which is a sphinx with her paw on a wheel.

We now ascend the staircase (A). View of Mariout. Those who are not tired of empty tombs will find plenty more to the right, down a stairway cut in the rock.

Immediately below Kom es Chogafa flows the *Mahmoudieh Canal,* made by Mohammed Ali (for the circumstances *see* p. 97). There is a road along it which leads, right, into the region of cotton warehouses. (Section VI).—To the left one can walk or drive all the way to Nouzha (Section IV). The route is partly pleasant

partly not. It crosses, at Moharrem Bey, the Farkha
Canal, which leaves the Mahmoudieh Canal at right
angles and which went all the way to the sea.—Fur-
ther on, there is a shady tract called the "Champs
Elysées"; it resembles, neither for good or evil, its
Parisian original.

SECTION IV

From the Square to Nouzha

ROUTE:—Take Nouzha Tram (Green Trefoil) at the lower end of the Boulevard Ramleh, just off the Square. The Rond Point Tram (White Star) passes through the Square, but does not go further than the Water Works—about halfway to Nouzha.

CHIEF POINTS OF INTEREST:—Municipal Gardens; Nouzha and Antoniadis Gardens.

For the Boulevard Ramleh *see* Section V. Having traversed it, the tram bears to the right and passes the Alhambra Theatre, the only one in the town—not a bad building.—Just beyond the Theatre a road leads left, to the Cathedral of the *Coptic Catholic Patriarchate* (p. 229), or Church of the Resurrection. The building is not remarkable, but of interest to all who would explore the ecclesiastical ramifications of Alexandria. It was dedicated in 1902 by the Patriarch Cyril II and endowed by the Emperor Francis Joseph of Austria, as an inscription by the entrance (shortly to be removed) states; the alternative date—1618—reckons by the Coptic Calendar, which begins not with the birth of Christ but with the persecutions of the 3rd cent. (p. 51). The façade of the church imitates that of St. John Lateran, Rome. Beyond the church are the British Consulate and the Egyptian Government Hospital (Section V).

The tram turns left, along the Rue Sultan Hussein, still popularly known as the Rue d'Allemagne, and passes between the Menasce Schools (Jewish) and Cromer Park, a small fenced garden reserved for ladies and babies.—*Place Said*, a round space in the midst of which is a large Ptolemaic Column, erected in memory of the retaking of Khartoum, Sept. 2, 1898; on each side of the column, statues of the lion headed goddess, Sekhet. The native women who sometimes sit in masses in the Place are professional mourners and await a funeral out of the Egyptian Government Hospital behind. Roads go from the Place: left, to Mazarita Station on the Ramleh tram line (Section V); right, to the Rue Rosette (Section I).

Left, the *Municipal Gardens*, small but admirably planned; the designer, M. Monfront, has shown real genius in his treatment of the area. The gardens follow the line of the Arab Walls (p. 86) and also cross the course of the old Farkha Canal that once connected the Mahmoudieh Canal and the sea (p. 168). Both these features have been utilised; the fortifications have turned into picturesque hillocks or survive as masses of masonry, which, though of little merit in themselves, have been cleverly grouped and look mediaeval by moonlight; while the water of the canal has been preserved in an artificial pool, the abode of ducks. The gardens should be thoroughly explored. In them— visible from tram—is a *Statue of Nubar Pasha*, by Puech; the tarboosh is too large but the general effect dignified; the left hand rests on a tablet inscribed "La justice est la base de tout Gouvernement," and the same maxim appears on the pedestal. Nubar was an Armenian—a politician whose honesty is variously estimated, though there is no question as to his ability. He became minister under the Khedive Ismail (1878) and tried to regulate his finance, also serving under

Tewfik. He was, as his favourite motto suggests, cautious in temperament. He is buried outside the Armenian Church (p. 156).

The tram touches the end of the Rue Rosette (Section I) and passes through the belt of the gardens: they continue on the right, still following the course of the vanished Arab Walls and utilising the acclivities, and are to be continued still further, as far as the railway station; they will then form a great horseshoe.—Left are the Roman Catholic Cemeteries, and in the second of these, at the end of the main walk, is a fine *Antique Tomb*, which should be seen. It lies in a hole; great walls of alabaster have fallen and exposed their shining surfaces. The shrine (Heroon) of Pompey stood near here, and it has been suggested that this was the actual place where his head was deposited after his murderers had brought it to Julius Caesar; this is pure conjecture, but the tomb may well date from the period (B.C. 48) for the work is very good.—To the right, in the new part of the Cemetery are other ancient tombs, also a cemented shaft with foot holds cut on its interior.

Almost opposite the entrance to the Cemetery is the War Memorial to French Soldiers, a truncated obelisk of Carrara marble, designed as a labour of love in memory of his fallen comrades by Mons. V. Erlanger, the French architect of Alexandria and unveiled April 23, 1921 by Lord Allenby.

The scroll facing the main thoroughfare bears the following inscription:

"In memory of French Soldiers fallen during the Great War and offered by members of the British Community to the French Colony to Commemorate the glorious deeds of arms, performed by the French Armies 1914–1918."

Now the tram turns, right, by the Rosetta Gate Police Station, surmounted by a turret clock in com-

memoration of King Edward VII, and comes to the
Rond Point, where are the Waterworks, and up the rise
Hadra Prison; then crosses the railway, the ancient
Hadra Cemetery (*see* Museum Room 19) and Hadra
village, and reaches its terminus at Nouzha, close to
Nouzha railway station and to the Mahmoudieh
Canal.

Nouzha was in Ptolemaic times the suburb of Eleusis.
Here lived Callimachus the poet (p. 33); here (B.C.
168) Popillius the Roman general checked the King of
Syria who was about to seize Alexandria, and, drawing
a circle round him in the sand, obliged him to decide
forthwith between peace and war. Here (A.D. 640),
were quartered the cavalry of Amr (p. 60), before he
entered the town.—The Gardens are across the railway.
They have been developed by the Municipality out of
a small park of Ismail's, and are most beautiful; if one
could judge Alexandria by her gardens one would do
nothing but praise. Some are formalised, others free;
those who like pelicans will find them in a pond to the
right; the zoological garden, a bandstand, and a restau-
rant, are straight ahead; view from over the top over
Lake Hadra towards Abou el Nawatir (Section V).—
Right of the bandstand is an enclosure entered by payment; this too should be visited as the trees and flowers
are fine; glasshouses also.

Above the pelican pond a small gate leads from the
Nouzha Gardens into the *Antoniadis Gardens* (entrance charge; varying according to the day of week).
These too belong to the Municipality of Alexandria.
They are full of modern statues, which, though of no
merit, make a pleasant formal effect. The trees and
creepers are fine, and there is a beautiful lawn at the
back of the house. Here, until recently, lived the Antoniadis family, wealthy Greeks.

In the field behind the Antoniadis Gardens is an
Antique Tomb. It is easiest reached through the back
gate, which a gardener will sometimes unlock; otherwise one must return to the Nouzha Gardens, pass out,
and follow the canal for a little way, finally turning to
the left. The tomb is behind an absurd spiral of rock-
work. It is reached down a flight of steps and the hall
is often under water. Same plan as at Anfouchi (p.
137); a sunken hall, out of which three tomb chambers
open.

The road beyond the Gardens, along the edge of the
Canal, is pretty, and probably follows the course of the
ancient Canal to Canopus, whither the Alexandrians
used to go out in barges, to enjoy themselves and to
worship Serapis. In one place it skirts the waters of
Hadra.

The other way (west) the Canal flows into the city
(Section II) finally entering the Harbour.—(For history of the Canal *see* p. 97.)

There is a road direct from Nouzha to Sidi Gaber
(Section V) by the side of the lake. It passes, left, the
place where two colossal statues were discovered: Antony as Osiris, and Cleopatra as Isis: Antony is in the
Museum (Garden Court, p. 132).

SECTION V

From the Square to Ramleh

ROUTE:—By the Boulevard Ramleh to the Tram Line terminus—10 min. walk. Then take tram with red label to Bulkeley, San Stefano, and Victoria. Tram with blue label goes to San Stefano only, *via* Bacos. The service is fair.

CHIEF POINTS OF INTEREST:—The Sea; the view from Abou el Nawatir; private gardens; the Spouting Rocks.

We start at the northeast corner of the Square, and take the Rue de l'Ancienne Bourse, in which are, right, the Union Club frequented by British, and, left, the former Bourse—the latter not a bad building, with a portico of marble columns and a vaulted interior; it is now the offices of the Lloyd Triestino. The street leads into the Boulevard Ramleh—turn to right.

The Boulevard (officially Rue de la Gare de Ramleh) is a busy shabby thoroughfare, full of people who are escaping to or from the tram terminus.

Right from Boulevard, in Rue Debbane, is a Greek and Syrian Catholic Church, dedicated to St. Peter (p. 229). It was built by Count Debbane, a Syrian under Brazilian protection who received his title from the Pope. His family vault extends along the whole length of the Chancel. The scene is of no interest, but typical of the complexities of religion and race at Alexandria.

Left from Boulevard, at end of Rue Averoff, is the Church of the Armenian Catholics (p. 228).

Right from Boulevard, in Rue de l'Eglise Copte, is the *Cathedral of the Coptic Orthodox Patriarchate* (p. 228) dedicated to St. Mark. Those who have never seen a Coptic Church should look in. It is fatuously ugly. On the screen that divides nave from sanctuary are several pictures—among them St. Damiana with her wheel; she is the native Egyptian Saint who was probably the origin of St. Catherine of Alexandria: round her are the forty maidens who shared her martyrdom. In the sanctuary are some pictures of St. Mark, whose primitive church is wrongly supposed to have stood on this site (p. 50); he is shown writing his Gospel or standing between Cleopatra's Needle and "Pompey's Pillar." Outside the Church are the Schools, ineptly adorned with a Lion of St. Mark of the Venetian type.

Right from Boulevard, the Rue Nebi Daniel leads past the chief Jewish Synagogue to the Rue Rosette (Section I).

The Boulevard reaches the tram terminus. To the right is the road to Nouzha (Section IV), to the left the sea and the New Quays (Section II).

On this featureless spot once arose a stupendous temple, the *Caesareum,* and a pair of obelisks, *Cleopatra's Needles.*

(i) HISTORY OF THE CAESAREUM. Cleopatra began it in honour of Antony (p. 28). After their suicide Octavian finished it in honour of himself (B.C. 13). He was worshipped there as Caesar Augustus, and the temple remained an Imperial possession until Christian times. Constantius II (A.D. 354) intended to present it to the Church, but before the transference could be effected St. Athanasius, who was always energetic, had held an Easter Service inside it. The

Emperor was offended. Two years later his troops nearly
killed Athanasius inside the building, and gave it to the
Arians. Arians and Orthodox continued to fight for and in
it and smashed it to pieces (p. 54). Athanasius, just back
from his final exile, built on the ruins a church which was
dedicated to St. Michael but usually retained the famous
title Caesareum. It became the Cathedral of Alexandria,
superseding St. Theonas (p. 50). Here in 415 Hypatia was
torn to pieces by tiles (p. 56). Here in 640 the Patriarch
Cyrus held a solemn service before betraying the city to
the Arabs (p. 60). Date of final destruction—912.

(ii). APPEARANCE. Nothing is known of the architecture
of the temple, but the Jewish philosopher Philo (p. 66)
thus writes of it in the day of its glory:

"It is a piece incomparably above all others. It stands
by a most commodious harbour: wonderful high and
large in proportion; an eminent sea-mark; full of choice
paintings and statues with donatives and oblatives in
abundance; and then it is beautiful all over with gold
and silver; the model curious and regular in the disposi-
tion of the parts, as galleries, libraries, porches, courts,
halls, walks, and consecrated groves, as glorious as expense and art could make them, and everything in the
proper place; besides that, the hope and comfort of sea-
faring men, either coming in or going out."

(iii). THE OBELISKS. In front of the Caesareum (between present tram terminus and sea) stood Cleopatra's
Needles of which one is now in the Central Park, New
York, and the other on the Embankment, London. They
had nothing to do with Cleopatra till after her death. They
were cut in the granite quarries of Assouan for Thothmes
III (B.C. 1500), and set up by him at Heliopolis near Cairo,
before the temple of the Rising Sun. In B.C. 13 they were
transferred here by the engineer Pontius. They rested not
directly on their bases but each on four huge metal crabs,
one of which has been recovered. Statues of Hermes or of
Victory tipped them. In the Arab period, when all around
decayed, they became the chief marvel of the city. One

fell. They remained in situ until the 19th cent., when they
were parted and took their last journey, the fallen one to
England in 1877, the other to the United States two years
later.

The walls of the Arab city used to reach the sea at
this point (cf. Belon's View, p. 89); they ended in a
tower that was swept away for the New Quays. We
now take the tram.

The first half mile of the tram lines traverses ground
of immense historical fame. Every inch was once sacred or royal. On the football fields to the left were the
Ptolemaic Palaces (p. 18) stretching down to the sea
and projecting into it at the Promontory of Lochias
(present Silsileh). There was also an island palace on
a rock that has disappeared. The walls of the Mouseion, too, are said to have extended into the area, but
we know no details and can only be certain that the
Ancient World never surpassed the splendour of the
scene. On the right, from the higher ground, the Theatre overlooked it, and the dramas of Aeschylus and
Euripides could be performed against the background
of a newer and a greater Greece. No eye will see that
achievement again, no mind can imagine it. Grit and
gravel have taken its place to-day.

Right of the line on leaving:—The British Consulate,
an imposing pile. Next to it, the *Egyptian Government
Hospital* probably on the site of the Ancient Theatre,
so a visit should be made. In the garden is the tomb
of Dr. Schiess a former Director; an early Christian
sarcophagus has been used, and on each side of it
are impressive Christian columns, probably from the
church of St. Theonas (p. 50) and each carved with a
cross in a little shrine. In the spiral ascent above the
tomb are other antiquities and a howitzer of Arabi's:

on the summit, an antique marble column, erected in memory of Queen Victoria's Jubilee.

MAZARITA STA.—A road leads, right, to the Public Gardens (Section IV) and, left, to the Promontory of Silsileh (*see* above). The promontory, like the rest of the coast, has subsided; in classical times it was broader and longer than now, and extended in breakwaters towards the Pharos (Fort Kait Bey), thus almost closing the entrance to the Eastern Harbour. The private port of the Ptolemies lay immediately to its left. A beacon, the Pharillon, was at its point in Arab times. The original Church of St. Mark, where the evangelist was buried, must have stood on the shore to its right. There is nothing to see to-day except a coast-guard station and the exit of the main drain.

CHATBY STA.—The tram has now pierced the ancient royal city and enters the region of the dead, where owing to the dryness of the ground the cemeteries both ancient and modern have been dug. Right, the modern cemeteries, Jewish nearest the tram line, behind them English, then Greek and Armenian, then Catholic, opening into the Aboukir road (Section I). Close to the sta. are the spacious schools of the Greek Community, and the Orwa el Woska schools. Left of the station, is the Sultanian Institute of Hydrobiology, containing a small but interesting aquarium and an extensive and valuable technical library, also models of fishing craft, nets and marine instruments. Visit by arrangement with the Director, Prof. Pachundaki. In the enclosure in front of the Institute some ancient Mosaics have been recently (1921) discovered; they are said to be of fine period and in good condition, but are not on exhibition yet; it is to be hoped that they will be accessible shortly. Traces of ancient roads and drains have also been found here.

CHATBY-LES-BAINS STA.—Turn left, as far as the fire station, then turn right. Here, in the waste to the left of the road, is the great Chatby Necropolis, the oldest in the Ptolemaic city (*see* Museum, particularly Room 20 and Garden Court). Little remains. There is a tomb-group close to the road of the Anfouchi type (p. 137) *i.e.* a sunken court out of which the burial places open; at the end of the tombs is a double sarcophagus of the shape of a bed, with cushions of stone. —Right of the tram line, other burial places, Ptolemaic and Roman, can be found all the way to the canal.— The tram goes through a cutting; right is the fine French Lycée, subsidized by the French Government.

CAMP DE CÉSAR STA.—Caesar never camped here. An unattractive suburb, anciently Eleusis by the Sea.

IBRAHAMIEH STA.—Then to the right, flat fertile land appears. This, geologically, is delta deposit, which has been silted up against the narrow spur of limestone on which Alexandria stands (p. 5). In the foreground, the green turf of the Sporting Club; further, the trees of Nouzha and the waters of Hadra. Traces of ancient Cemeteries continue on the dry ground on the left.

SPORTING CLUB STA.—Close to the Grand Stand of the Race Course. Bathing beach left.

CLEOPATRA STA.—Cleopatra never lived here. Right begin the famous fig trees of Sidi Gaber, reputed the best in Egypt. Also broad leaved bananas, maize, &c. A pleasant road leads across the railway and by the side of the lake to Nouzha Gardens (Section IV); it can be beautiful here in the evening.—Left from the sta., at the base of a cliff by the edge of the sea, is a Ptolemaic tomb with painted walls, but even while one describes such things they are being destroyed. The reefs by this tomb form the pretty little "Friars' pool."

Sidi Gaber Sta.—Close to the main-line railway sta. where all the Cairo expresses stop.—Left, a road leads between fine trees to the *Abercrombie Monument*, a poor affair, but interesting to Englishmen, as it commemorates our exploits in 1801 (p. 93). It is a three-sided column of white marble, surmounted by a flaming urn. Inscription:

"To the memory of Sir Ralph Abercrombie K.B.&C. and the Officers and Men who fell at the battle of Alexandria, March 21st, 1801 . . . . . As his life was honourable so was his death glorious. His memory will be recorded in the annals of his country—will be sacred to every British soldier—and embalmed in the recollection of a grateful posterity."

Close to the Monument is the modern Mosque of Sidi Gaber, a beneficent local saint, who flies about at night, looks after children, &c.

Mustapha Pacha Sta.—Right, up the road, is the hill of Abou el Nawatir, the highest near Alexandria, overlooking the lakes of Hadra and Mariout; exquisite view, especially by evening light. The square enclosure at the top belongs to the reservoir; to its S.E. half-way between it and the railway, a *Gun* lies in the sand. This is a relic of the fighting of July 1882. General Alison placed most of his artillery up here (p. 102), and the gun still points to the Mahmoudieh Canal, in the direction of Arabi's camp.—Left of Mustapha Pacha Sta. on the rise, are the British Barracks, occupying the site of the Roman; history repeats herself, just as she has done in the Cemeteries. Octavian's town of Nicopolis, which he founded in B.C. 30 to overawe Alexandria (p. 48), began here. Among the Roman Units here quartered were the 2nd Trajana Fortis and the 3rd Cyrenaic; the British are too numerous to record.

CARLTON STA.—The big Villa up the hill to the right was built by a German in the Greek style, regardless of expense or taste.

BUCKELEY STA.—We are now in the heart of Ramleh ("Sand") the straggling suburb where the British and other foreigners reside. Lovely private gardens, the best in Egypt. Left of the sta. is Stanley Bay, a fine bit of coast scenery and a favourite bathing place: also the Anglican Church of All Saints (p. 230).

The tram line here divides into two branches that reunite at San Stefano. The left branch—more direct—goes by Saba Pacha (pretty cove in coast), Glymenopoulo, Mazloum, Zizinia—all bathing places. The right branch, through pretty palm groves, via Fleming, Bacos, Seffer, Schutz, Gianaclis (left is the fine new Mosque of Ahmed Pacha Yehia, the statesman, with provision for his tomb).

SAN STEFANO STA.—Close to the Casino, a fashionable summer hotel, by the side of a sea that seems especially fresh and blue. There are Symphony concerts here in the season. The audience however comes not to listen but to talk; their noise is so great that from a little distance the orchestra appears to be performing in dumb show.

The tram goes on by St. George, Laurens and Palais stations to Sidi Bishr, on the edge of a desert coast. Fine walk or ride past Sidi Bishr Mosque to the *Spouting Rocks*. These are most remarkable. Masses of limestone project into the sea, which penetrates beneath them and spouts up through blow holes and cracks. Some of the vents have been artificially squared, and the Ancient Alexandrians, who loved scientific toys, may have fitted them up with musical horns or mechanical mills.—The expedition may be continued along the coast to the woods of Montazah (Section VII).

VICTORIA STA.—The terminus. Here is a Ry. sta. for the Aboukir and Rosetta lines (Section VII), also Victoria College, a huge building. It offers an education on English Public School lines to residents in Egypt, whatever their creed or race, and was much approved by Lord Cromer, who founded a scholarship here.

The coast walk from Alexandria to Ramleh is rarely taken but is charming—low crumbly cliffs, sandy beaches, flat rocks, and vestiges of ancient houses and tombs that help one to realise how the whole site of the city has sunk. There is no road east of Silsileh. The scheme for a grandiose "Corniche" drive has fortunately failed, and the scenery has escaped the standardised dulness that environs most big towns.

Ramleh can also be reached by the Aboukir Road, an extension of the Rue Rosette (Section I).

SECTION VI

From the Square to Mex

ROUTE:—By the Rue des Soeurs and Gabbari, taking the Mex Tram (White Star). The journey is uncomfortable and uninspiring, but Mex is pleasant.

We start from the south side of the Square, down the long Rue des Soeurs, which takes its name from the Roman Catholic Convent and School near its entrance. The surroundings become squalid.

Right of Rue des Soeurs:—Rue Behari Bey leads to the mound of *Kom-el-Nadoura,* which rises abruptly out of mean streets. Its history before the arrival of Napoleon (1798 p. 91) is unknown. His engineer Cafarelli fortified it for him, and it held back the British advance in 1801, (p. 93). The entrance is on the south side, through a doorway by a winding path fringed with prickly pear and pepper trees. The summit—104 feet above the sea—is now used as a signalling station and observatory under the Ports and Lights Administration. Interesting set of instruments, and fine view of harbour and city. At the N.N.W. corner are some remains of Cafarelli's masonry.—Outside the Fort, in the Rue Bab-el-Akhdar (Section II) is the Gold and Silver Bazaar.

Left of Rue des Soeurs is the Genenah, a curious rabbit warren.

The tram passes down Rue Ibrahim Premier. To the right, close to the docks, in the Rue Karam, is a Franciscan church and school. They are modern and of no interest, but stand on a site that was important historically. Here was the *Church of St. Theonas* (p. 50) and the early palace of the bishops. Here St. Athanasius was brought up. The Arabs (641) incorporated what they found into a fine Mosque, called the Mosque of the Seventy (from some fallacious connection with the Septuagint) or the Mosque of the 1,000 Columns. It was on the lines of the Mosque of Ibn Touloun at Cairo; the Rue Karam bisects its area; its prayer niche faced southwest. It was standing in a ruined condition when the French came, and was turned into artillery barracks.

Just before the tram reaches the Canal we pass, right, the cotton exchange of Minet-el-Bassal. A visit— introduction necessary—is interesting. The Exchange is round a pleasant courtyard, with a fountain in the midst. Samples are exhibited. The whole neighbourhood is given up to this, the main industry, of Alexandria; warehouses; picturesque wooden machinery for cleaning the cotton and pressing it into bales; in the season, the streets are slippery with greasy fluff.

The Mahmoudieh Canal (p. 97) is now crossed. The banks have here their original stone casings and double descents, recalling the commercial enterprise of Mohammed Ali. A walk along the banks to the left is dirty but attractive; it can terminate at the Kom-es-Chogafa Catacombs (Section III). Right, the Canal enters the Western Harbour.

Then comes the district of Gabbari, called after a sheikh of that name. Here was the Western Cemetery of the Ancient City; the finds have been taken to the Museum (Room 14). Nothing interesting until Mex.

Mex, once a fishing village, might have become a

prosperous suburb of Alexandria, like Ramleh. But the intervening slums have choked access to it. It lies midway on the big curve of the Western Harbour, the waters of Lake Mariout being close behind. There is a good pier, with a wooden causeway that leads on to a distant rock. The little sea front has rather a Neapolitan air.

Beyond Mex are the limestone quarries that provided the stone for the ancient and the modern towns. They are cut in the ridge that here separates lake and sea.

The village of Dekhela lies further along the beach. Fine walk from it to Amrieh (Section VIII). Beyond it the desert begins, strewn with fragments of antique pottery.

Beyond Dekhela, at the western point of the Harbour: *Fort Agame*. A strategic point in Napoleonic times (p. 91) and in the Bombardment of Alexandria (p. 100). Magnificent bathing. Just off the Fort is *Marabout Island,* so called from the tomb of a local saint which stands here, adorned with votive models of boats. Makrizi (writing in the 14th cent.) says that men lived longer on Marabout Island than anywhere else in the world, but no one at all lives here now. From it extends the chain of reefs that close the entrance of the Western Harbour (p. 6).—It is easy to visit this district from Alexandria by sailing boat, but not easy to get back again in the evening when the wind drops.

SECTION VII

Aboukir and Rosetta

ROUTE:—By train from the Main (Cairo) sta., or from Sidi-Gaber, where all trains stop, and which is also a sta. for the Ramleh Tram (Section VI).

CHIEF POINTS OF INTEREST:—Montazah; Canopus; Aboukir Bay; Rosetta.

At Sidi Gaber sta. is a view of Lake Hadra on the right.—Five stations on:—Victoria, close to the College and tram terminus.—The train passes over sand and through a palm oasis, which is carpeted with flowers in spring.

MANDARAH STA.—One of the houses in the village is painted outside in commemoration of the inmate's pilgrimage to Mecca—pictures of things that he saw or would like to have seen, such as a railway train, a tiger, a siren, and a very large melon.

MONTAZAH STA.—Close to the station is the *Summer Resort* of the ex-Khedive Abbas II, now (1922) being restored and refurnished by King Fouad. Permission to enter should be obtained if possible, for the scenery is unique in Egypt and of the greatest beauty. The road leads by roses, oleanders and pepper trees. From it a road turns, right, up the hill to the Selamlik (men's

COUNTRY ROUND ALEXANDRIA

Scale of English Miles

0   10   20

MEDITERRANEAN

SEA

Rosetta mouth of Nile

Rosetta

NILE

Nelson I.

Aboukir

Edkou

Montazah

Ramleh

LAKE EDKOU

ALEXANDRIA

Mahmoudieh Canal

Agame

Mex

LAKE MARIOUT

Abousir

Damanhour

To Cairo

Amrieh

Ikingi Mariout

Bahig

Boundary between Delta

Gharbaniat

and Desert

Hammam

To Dagba

St. Menas

LIBYAN

WADY NATRUN

DESERT

Lakes

Bir Hooker

To Khatatbeh

St. Baramus

Convent of the Syrians

St. Pschoi

St. Macarius

Lakes summer levels
"   winter   "

quarters), built by the Khedive in a style that was likely to please his Austrian mistress; on the terrace in front is a sun dial and some guns. From the terrace, *View* of the circular bay with its fantastic promontories and breakwaters; the coast to the right is visible as far as Aboukir, whose minaret peeps over a distant headland; to the left are the Montazah woods; beneath, down precipitous steps, a curved parade. Beautiful walks in every direction, and perfect bathing. On the promontory to the right is a kiosk, and at its point are some remains of buildings or baths—fragments of the ancient Taposiris Parva that once stood here; some of them form natural fishponds. The woods are Pines Maritimes, imported by the Khedive from Europe, and in the western section, beyond the Pigeon House, the trees have grown high. Various buildings are in the estate; in one corner are the foundations of an enormous mosque. During the recent war (1914–1919) Montazah became a Red Cross Hospital; thousands of convalescent soldiers passed through it and will never forget the beauty and the comfort that they found there.

MAMOURAH STA.—The low ground to the right is on the site of the Aboukir Lake (p. 92), drained in the 19th cent. Here the Aboukir and Rosetta railways part.

ABOUKIR

ROUTE:—Aboukir Station is the terminus. Walk or take donkey. Turn sharply to the left to Canopus, 1 mile, then follow coast all the way round by Fort Kait Bey to Fort Ramleh; return to Aboukir Village.

Aboukir, though intimately connected with Alexandria, has a history of its own. Three main periods.

ABOUKIR AND DISTRICT

MEDITERRANEAN SEA

Nelson's course Aug. 1st 1798

Culloden (wrecked)

The Vanguard (Nelson's Flagship)

The Orient (Bruey's Flagship)

British

French Position

British

Nelson Island

BAY OF ABOUKIR

Ft. Kait Bey (Cape Zephyrium) (Ch. of S.S. Cyr and John)

ABOUKIR Village

(MENOUTHIS)

(HERACLEUM) (Ancient exit of NILE) (Canopic Mouth)

Ft. Ramleh (Waterworks)

*Baths of Cleopatra

To Rosetta

Ft. Saba

Catacombs Sta.

Catacombs Fragments

Ft. Serapis

T. of Serapis (Canopus)

Ft. Tewfikieh

Aerodrome Sta.

(Course of Canopic Canal?)

Lower Baths

Upper Baths

Island

Lake Aboukir (drained)

To Alex.

(i). ANCIENT (*see* also p. 7).

Geologically, this is the end of the long limestone spur that projects from the Libyan desert (p. 5). The Nile had to round it to reach the sea, and it is to the Nile that its early fame is due. The river poured out just to the east, through the "Canopic" Mouth, which has now dried up, and there were settlements here centuries before Alexandria was founded. On the left bank of the Nile (south of the present Fort Ramleh) Herodotus (B.C. 450) saw a temple to Heracles, and was told that Paris and Helen had sought shelter here on their flight to Troy—shelter that was refused by the local authorities, who disapproved of their irregular union. There was a second settlement at Menouthis (Fort Ramleh itself), and a third and most famous at *Canopus* (present Fort Tewfikieh), from which the whole district took its name.

Canopus, according to Greek legend, was a pilot of Menelaus who was bitten here by a serpent as they returned from Troy, and, dying, became the tutelary God. The legend, like that of Paris and Helen, shows how interested were the Greeks in the district, but has no further importance. There is also a legend that Canopus was an Egyptian God whose body was an earthenware jar: this too may be discredited. With the foundation of Alexandria (B.C. 331) the district lost much of its trade, but became a great fashionable and religious resort. There was a canal from Alexandria, probably connecting with the Nile just where it entered the sea, and the Alexandrians glided along it in barges, singing and crowned with flowers. In connection with his new cult of Serapis (p. 20) Ptolemy Soter built a temple here (*see* below) whose fame spread over the world and whose rites made the Romans blush with shame or pale with envy; here originated the idea, still so widely held in the west, that Egypt is a land of licentiousness and mystery. The district decayed as soon as Christianity was established; it had not, like Alexandria, a solid basis for its existence in trade. But Paganism lingered here, and as late as the end of the 5th century twenty camel-loads of idols were found secreted in a house and were carried away to make a bonfire at Alexandria. Demons gave trouble even in later times.

(ii). CHRISTIAN.

The Patriarch Cyril (p. 56) having destroyed the cults of Serapis and Isis in the district (A.D. 389) sent out the relics of St. Cyr to take their place. The relics were so intermingled with those of another martyr, St. John, that St. John had to be brought too, and a church to them both arose just to the south of the present Fort Kait Bey. The two Saints remained quiet for 200 years, but then began to disentangle themselves and work miracles, and recovered for the district some of its ancient popularity; indeed many of their cures are exactly parallel to those effected in the Temple of Serapis. With the Arab invasion their church vanishes, but St. Cyr has given his name to modern Aboukir ("Father Cyr"). In the 9th century the Canopic branch of the Nile dried up. The Turks built some forts here for coastal defence, but history does not recommence until the arrival of Nelson.

(iii). MODERN.

In Napoleonic times Aboukir saw two great battles.

(a). "Battle of the Nile."

For the event that led to this engagement *see* p. 91. Brueys, Napoleon's admiral, brought his fleet into the bay for safety, and anchored them in a long line, about two miles from the coast. He had 13 Men-of-War, 4 Frigates, 1,182 cannons, and 8,000 men. To the north was "Nelson's Island," as it is now called, which he had fortified and upon which his line was supposed to rest. His flagship, the *Orient*, was midway in the line. He took up this position on July 7th, 1798.

On August 1st Nelson arrived in pursuit, with 14 Men-of-War, 1,012 cannons and 8,068 men. The wind was N.W., a usual direction in summer. Half his fleet, including his flagship the *Vanguard*, attacked Brueys from the expected quarter, the east. The other half, led by the *Goliath*, executed the brilliant manœuvre that brought us victory. It gave Brueys a double surprise: in the first place it passed between the head of his line and "Nelson's Island" where he thought there was no room; in the second place it took up a position to his west, between him and the shore, where he thought the water was too shallow. Thus he was caught between two fires—attacked by the whole British Fleet with the exception of the *Culloden,* which, sailing too near "Nelson's Island", stranded.

The engagement began at 6.0 p.m. At 7.0 Brueys was killed, at 9.30 the *Orient* caught fire and blew up shortly afterwards; the explosion was tremendous and terminated the first act of the battle; an interval of appalled silence ensued. Casabianca was sailing the *Orient,* and it was on her "burning deck" that the boy of Mrs. Hemans' poem stood. The fighting recommenced, continuing through the night, and ending at midday on the 2nd with the complete victory of Nelson. The French fleet had been annihilated; only two Men-of-War and two Frigates escaped, and Napoleon had lost for ever his command of the Mediterranean. Nelson accordingly signalled the following message:—

> Almighty God having blessed His Majesty's arms with victory, the Admiral intends returning public thanksgiving for the same at two o'clock this day, and he recommends every ship doing the same as soon as convenient.

The French expected an attack on Alexandria, but Nelson had suffered too much himself to attempt this; having rested for a little, he dispersed his fleet, leaving only a few ships behind to watch the coast. In his despatches home he stated that the engagement had taken place not far from the (Rosetta) mouth of the Nile; hence the official "Battle of the Nile" instead of the more accurate "Naval Battle of Aboukir."

(b). Land Battle of Aboukir.

Less important than its predecessor, but the strategy is interesting, and Napoleon himself was present. For the events that led up to it *see* p. 92; Turkey, at the instigation of England, had declared war on France, and in July 1799 the Turks occupied Aboukir Bay and landed 15,000 men.

Their left rested on the present Fort Ramleh, their right on the present Fort Tewfikieh, their camp was in the narrow extremity of the peninsula, between the redoubt and the Fort at the very tip. They were supported on three sides by their fleet, which was stationed in the Mediterranean, in the Bay of Aboukir, and in the (vanished) Lake of Aboukir. From this stronghold they proposed to overrun Egypt.

On receiving the news, Napoleon hurried down from Cairo and arrived (July 25th) with only 10,000 men, mostly cavalry. Murat and Kléber accompanied him. He began by clearing the Turkish gunboats out of Lake Aboukir; then his force attacked Forts Ramleh and Tewfikieh, while his cavalry under Murat, advancing over the level ground between them, drove the flying defenders of each into the Mediterranean and the Bay respectively. 5,400 Turks were drowned. The tip of the peninsula remained and resisted vigorously, but Napoleon managed to mount some of his guns on the hard spit of sand that still extends along the shore of the Bay, and thus to cannonade the Turkish Camp, which was finally taken by storm.

RUINS OF CANOPUS.

The ruins (*see* above) lie round Fort Tewfikieh which is seen to the left as the train runs into the station. They were once of interest, but have been almost entirely destroyed by the military authorities, who use the limestone blocks for road making, and allow treasure hunting to go on. The remains are not easy to find, as the area is pitted with excavations. Consult map.

(*a*). About 50 yds. from the gateway of the fort, in a hollow to the left of the road, are two huge *Fragments* of a granite temple. Here were found the busts of Rameses II in the Museum (Room 7) and the colossi of the same King and his daughter (Museum, Court). Date of statues:—B.C. 1300.

(*b*). Further to the left, round the Fort, is the site

of the *Temple of Serapis,* the most famous building on
the peninsula, and celebrated throughout the antique
world. It was dedicated by Ptolemy III Euergetes (p.
17) and his wife Berenice. A few years later (B.C. 238)
their baby daughter died, and the priests met here in
conclave to make her a goddess, and incidentally to
endorse some reforms in the Calendar that the King,
who had a scientific mind, was pressing. The pro-
nouncement has been preserved in the "Decree of
Canopus," now one of the chief documents for Ptolemaic history. As for miracles, the temple even out-
stripped the original Temple of Serapis at Alexandria:
invalids who slept here even by proxy discovered next
day that they were well. It was also the abode of magic
and licentiousness according to its enemies, and of philosophy according to its friends. Christianity attacked
it. Just before its destruction (A.D. 289) Antoninus, an
able pagan reactionary, settled here, and tried to re-
vive the cult. "Often he told his disciples that after his
time there would be no temple, and that the great and
venerable sanctuary would remain only as an unmeaning mass of ruins, forgotten by all." (Eunapius, life of
Edesius). Antoninus was right.

In ancient time the Temple probably stood on the
highest ground, but with the general rising of level the
site is now in a deep depression and must be hunted
for patiently. An oblong space has been cleared and
some columns and capitals from the excavations have
been ranged round it, but it is impossible to reconstruct the original plan, and much has yet to be un-
earthed. Indeed it is not quite certain that this is the
right temple; an inscription has been discovered dedi-
cating it not to Serapis but to Osiris—with whom however Serapis was often identified. The columns are of
granite or of stucco-coated limestone. Beneath the
broken tin shelter was once a pretty mosaic. The finest

object is a stupendous fluted column of red granite that lies in a pit close by; no use for it has yet occurred to the military authorities. To the south and east of the Temple were the houses of the priests, showing fine cemented passages; these have been destroyed.

The canal by which revellers and worshippers approached this shrine ran to the south, through the low land by the railway; its course is uncertain; its exit was either into the (vanished) Nile, or into Aboukir Bay.

(c). *The Upper Baths.*—These lie about 100 yds. nearer the sea, on the slope just above the corner of the great bay that stretches to Montazah (p. 186). When excavated a few years ago they were almost perfect. The swimming bath—lined with the hard pink cement that indicates Ptolemaic or Roman work—had at the top a double step for the bathers. All round its sides were inserted large earthenware pots, their mouths level with the surface. Of this unique building a small fragment now survives. The brick central cistern and the hot baths can also still be traced.

(d). *The Lower Baths and Broken Colossus.*—Continuing to round Fort Tewfikieh we reach the coast and follow it N.E. Awash with the sea are the foundations of some large baths, showing the entrance channels which were probably closed with sluices, also some grooves of unknown use. On the shore above are the hot baths of the same establishment, retaining traces of pink cement. In the surf to the left lie blocks of granite: closely inspected, they resolve into fragments of a Colossus (Rameses II ?) and a sphinx.

(e). *Catacombs.*—Fifty yards on, at a point about halfway between the coast and the fort are a couple of catacombs, lying each of them in a hollow. One has a subterranean room, the other a sarcophagus slide. Traces of tombs and tunnels all over the area and along the low cliff by the shore.

This completes our survey of Canopus, once so en-
chanting a spot. Of its ancient delights only the air and
the sea remain.

Continue to follow the coast. Perfect bathing. To the
right, halfway between the coast and the railway sta.
in some rising ground, are catacombs that have been
filled in. Then comes the end of the promontory, which
is fine. There are two forts:—Fort Saba, closing the
neck, where the French resisted when the Turks
landed in 1799 (*see* above); and Fort Kait Bey, on the
extremity, founded in the 15th cent. by the Sultan of
that name as part of his defence scheme against the
Turks (cf. Fort Kait Bey at Alexandria, p. 87). The
views are good, with the Mediterranean on one side
and the tranquil semicircle of Aboukir Bay on the
other, and from here or from Fort Ramleh the scene
of the "Battle of the Nile" can be surveyed, and Nelson's great manoeuvre appreciated; "Nelson's Island"
from which the French line depended and where
the Culloden was wrecked lies straight ahead (*see*
above). The promontory was anciently called Zephyrium, because it caught the cool zephyr winds; here
stood a little temple to Aphrodite and when the great
queen Arsinoe died in B.C. 270, one of the court ad-
mirals had the happy idea of associating her with the
elder goddess so that mariners might render thanks to
both. The shrine then became fashionable and Queen
Berenice hung up her hair here in 244 as a thank-
offering for her husband's safe return; in the following
year the hair was snatched up to heaven, where it may
still be observed on any fine night as the constellation
of Coma Berenice. The temple was less fortunate, and
all that remains of it is the base of a column, down
among the rocks.—In Christian times the Church of St.

Cyr and St. John (*see* above) stood here, on the side of Aboukir Bay.

Aboukir Bay.—The shore is airless and there are palm trees, the waters shallow. From a boat one can look down on the mud in which the Orient, Brueys' flagship, has disappeared with all her treasure; attempts have been made to locate her, but in vain. Good sailing. Turtle fishing. On the projecting spit to which Napoleon dragged his guns (*see* above) is the landing enclosure for the fishing boats; many of the fishermen are Sicilians; they have lived at Aboukir for generations and form a community by themselves. Here (site uncertain) once stood Menouthis.

Fort Ramleh.—Topped by the waterworks. Magnificent view. The flat ground to the south marks the Canopic Mouth of the Nile, through which Herodotus entered Egypt; here Heracleum stood (*see* above).

About quarter mile S.W. of Fort Ramleh, and close to a small modern pumping tower, are the so-called *Baths of Cleopatra.* She had nothing to do with them, but they are worth seeing. The western outer wall, of limestone blocks, is well preserved. Steps lead up through it. Within are pavements of pebble mosaic, fragments of stucco, a stone with a drain groove, &c. In a chamber to the left, is an oblong bath nearly six feet deep; steps lead down to it and in the centre of its pebbled floor is a little depression; in the edge of the brim and on the wall opposite are niches, as if to support beams, and provision for the entrance and exit of the water can also be seen. Further on, past a small stucco cistern, is an entrance to a small room which contains an oblong bath to lie down in, quite modern and suburban in appearance; close to it, under a niche, is a footbath—the bather sat on a seat which has disappeared but whose supports can be seen.—These baths are all in the western part of the enclosure; the rest contains other and larger chambers but is in worse preservation. It is much to be wished that these baths, which have been recently excavated, could be protected properly; otherwise they will share the fate of the other antiquities within the military zone.

Aboukir Village, to which we return through palm trees, contains nothing of note.

On leaving Mamourah Junction (p. 188) the railway to Rosetta bears to the right, and crosses the salt marshy ground over which the Canopic branch of the Nile once flowed to the sea. Rural Egypt can be seen at last. Beyond El Tarh station the train crosses a bit of Lake Edku; view of the village to the left.

Edku (no hotel or café) stands on a high mound between the lake and the Mediterranean. The houses in its steep streets are of red brick strengthened with courses of palm and other woods; they anticipate the more complicated architecture of Rosetta; there are some carved doors, Italianate in style. Mosques, unimportant. On the top of the ridge are some eight sailed windmills; they grind corn. Fine date palms grow on the sand dunes towards the sea, for there is fresh water just beneath the surface. There is an interesting local weaving industry, chiefly of silk, imported in its rough state from China. The work rooms are generally on the upper floors of the houses, and reached by an outside staircase. Quiet pleasant places; on the walls of some are Cufic inscriptions, inlaid in brick. The weavers sit to their looms in small oval pits; they have the hands of craftsmen and produce on their simple wooden machinery fabrics that are both durable and beautiful.

Fish are caught in Lake Edku. Some of the fishermen wade far into shallow waters; there is also a fleet of boats which moor to the long wooden jetty by the station. Occasional flamingoes.

The railway continues between lake and sea, finally bending northward and curving round great groves of palm trees, behind which lie the town of Rosetta and the river Nile.

ROSETTA

Rosetta and Alexandria are rivals; when one rises the other declines. Rosetta, situated on the Nile, would have dominated but for an overwhelming drawback; she has, and can have, no sea-harbour, because the coast in this part of Egypt is mere delta; the limestone ridges that created the two harbours of Alexandria do not continue eastward of Aboukir. Alexandria required organising by human science, but once organised she was irresistible. It is only in an unscientific age that Rosetta has been important. Let us briefly examine the birth and death, rebirth and decay, of civilisation here.

(i). In Pharaonic times the town and river-port of *Bolbitiné* were built hereabouts—probably a little up stream, beyond the present mosque of Abou Mandour. Nothing is known of the history of Bolbitiné. When Alexandria was founded (B.C. 331) traffic deserted the "Bolbitiné" mouth of the Nile for the "Canopic" and for the Alexandrian harbours, and the town decayed consequently. Its chief memorial is the so-called "Rosetta Stone," a basalt inscription now in the British Museum. The inscription enumerates the merits of King Ptolemy V Epiphanes (B.C. 196; *see* genealogical tree p. 14). It is a dull document, a copy of the original decree which was set up at Memphis and reproduced broadcast over the country. But it is important because it is written in three scripts—Hieroglyphic, Demotic and Greek—and thus led to the deciphering of the ancient Egyptian language. The antique columns &c., that may be seen in Rosetta to-day also probably came from

Bolbitiné. But it was never important, and the sands have now covered it.

(ii). *Rosetta* itself was founded in A.D. 870 by El Motaouakel, one of the Abbaside Caliphs of Egypt. The date is most significant. By 870 the Canopic mouth of the Nile had dried up, and isolated Alexandria from the Egyptian water system. Shipping passed back to the Bolbitiné mouth, and frequented it again for nearly a thousand years. "El Raschid" as the Arabs named the new settlement, became the western port of Egypt, Damietta being the eastern. It was important in the Crusades; St. Louis of France (1049) knew it as "Rexi." In the 17th and 18th centuries it was practically rebuilt in its present form; the mosques, dwelling houses, cisterns, the great warehouses for grain that line the river bank, all date from this period. It evolved an architectural style, suitable to the locality. The chief material is brick, made from the Nile mud, and coloured red or black, there was no limestone to hand, such as supplied Alexandria: with the bricks are introduced courses of palm wood, antique columns &c., and a certain amount of mashrabiyeh work and faience. The style is picturesque rather than noble and may be compared with the brick style of the North German Hansa towns. Examples of it are to be found throughout the Delta and even in Alexandria herself (p. 136), but Rosetta is its headquarters. In architecture, as in other matters, the town kept in touch with Cairo; an Oriental town, scarcely westernised even today. So long as Alexandria lay dormant, it flourished; at the beginning of the 19th century its population was 35,000, that of Alexandria 5,000.

In 1798 Napoleon's troops took Rosetta, in 1801 the British and Turks retook it, in 1807 the reconnoitering expedition of General Frazer (p. 94) was here repulsed. These events, unimportant in themselves, were the prelude to an irreparable disaster: the revival of Alexandria, on scientific lines, by Mohammed Ali. As soon as he developed the harbours there and restored the connection with the Nile water systems by cutting the Mahmoudieh Canal, (p. 97), Rosetta began to decay exactly as Bolbitiné had decayed two thousand years before. The population now is 14,000 as against Alexandria's 400,000, and it has become wizen and puny through inbreeding. The warehouses and mosques are falling down, the costly private dwellings of the merchants have been gutted, and the sand, advancing from the south and from the west, invades a little farther every year through the palm groves and into the streets. One can wander aimlessly for hours (it is best thus to wander) and can see nothing that is modern, nor anything more exciting than the arrival of the fishing fleet with sardines. It is the East at last, but the East outwitted by science, and in the last stages of exhaustion.

The main street of Rosetta starts from the Railway Station and runs due south, parallel to the river, so it is easy to find one's way. In it is the only hotel, kept by a Greek; those who are not fastidious can sleep here: the rest must manage to see the sights between trains. The hotel has a pleasant garden, overlooked by the minaret of a mosque.

In the main street, to the right;—*Mosque of Ali-el-Mehalli,* built 1721, but containing the tomb of the Saint, who died in the 16th century. A large but uninteresting building, with an entrance porch in the "Delta" style—bricks arranged in patterns, pendentives, &c.

Further down, to the left, by the covered bazaars: Entrance with old doors to a large ruined building, probably once an "okel" or courtyard for travellers and their animals; one can walk through it and come out the other side through a fine portal, in the direction of the river. All this part of the town is most picturesque. The houses are four or five stories high, and have antique columns fantastically disposed among their brickwork. The best and oldest example of this domestic architecture is the *House of Ali-el-Fatairi,* in the Haret-el-Ghazl, with inscriptions above its lintels that date it 1620; its external staircase leads to two doors, those of the men's and women's apartments respectively. Other fine houses are those of:—Cheikh Hassan el Khabbaz in Rue Dahliz el Molk; Osman Agha, at some cross roads,—carved wood inside, date 1808; Ahmed Agha in the Chareh el Ghabachi to the west of the town, invaded by sand.

At the end of the main street is the most important building in the town, the *Mosque of Zagloul*. It really consists of two mosques: the western was founded about 1600 by Zagloul, the Mameluke or body-servant of Said Hassan; the other and more ruinous section is the Mosque of El Diouai. There is a courtyard with fountain in centre. The entire mass measures about 80 by 100 yds. All is brick except the two stone minarets; the ruined one was "cut with scissors" according to local opinion, but according to archaeology fell in the early 19th cent. The sanctuary of the Mosque of Zagloul proper is a stupendous hall; over 300 columns, many of them antique, are arranged in six parallel rows, there are four praying niches, three of them elaborately decorated, there is the tomb of the ex-body-servant himself, now worshipped as a saint and wooed by votive offerings of boats, and, in the tomb, his former master, the Said Hassan, lies with him, and shares his honours. The sanctuary is ruinous and carelessly built, but its perspective effects, especially from the south wall, near the tomb, are very fine and rival those of the Mosque of El Azhar at Cairo. Light enters through openings in the roof.

East of the Mosque of Zagloul and close to the river is the Mosque of *Mohammed el Abbas*, date 1809, of superior construction but on the same style; it has, unlike the other mosques of Rosetta, a fine dome, covering the tomb of the saint.

Other Mosques:—Toumaksis Mosque, built by Saleh Agha Toumaksis in 1694; it is reached up steps; fine iron work round the key holes; there is a good pulpit inside, also tiles, and the prayer niche retains its original geometrical decoration of hexagons and "Solomon's seals."—Mosque of Cheikh Toka, which stands in an angle of the Chareh Souk el Samak el Kadim; portal in "Delta" style with rosace over its arches; inside, pulpit dated 1727.

About a mile to the south of the town, best reached by boat, is the *Mosque of Abou Mandour*, a showy modern building, well placed on the bend of the river bank, and backed by huge sand hills that threaten to bury it, as they have buried Bolbitiné.

North of the town, and halfway between it and the sea, is the site of Fort St. Julien, which Napoleon's soldiers built, and where they discovered the Rosetta Stone. The Fort has disappeared; there is a sketch of it in the Alexandria Museum (Vestibule).

Sailing on the Nile: delightful.

SECTION VIII

The Libyan Desert

ROUTES:—By the Mariout Railway to Bahig for Abousir and for St. Menas; each expedition takes a day.

By Railway *via* Tel el Baroud and Khatatbeh to the Wady Natrun; 2 or 3 days.

Alexandria, though so cosmopolitan, lies on the verge of civilisation. Westward begins an enormous desert of limestone that stretches into the heart of Africa. The very existence of this desert is forgotten by most of the dwellers in the city, but it has played a great part in her history, especially in Christian times, and no one who would understand her career can ignore it.

The Mariout Railway was originally the property of the ex-Khedive. The line starts from the central station and diverges from the main line at Hadra. Having passed Nouzha Station (Section IV) it crosses the Mahmoudieh Canal (p. 97), then bends westward along the edge of Lake Mariout. Just before Gabbari Garden Station is a fishing village built on a tiny creek and quite Japanese in appearance. It is worth going down here when there has been a catch: the lake fish are uncanny monsters. The neighbourhood is very fertile—palms, bananas and vegetable gardens. But it does not make pleasant walking owing to the smells.

Mex Station (Section VI). The train crosses the western or Mellaha arm of Mariout. Right, are the salt pans that turn dull purple and red in the summer; beyond them the white spur of limestone that divides lake from sea.

Abd el Kader Station. Now we approach the Libyan Desert. The scenery and the people change. From the hill to the right, by the tomb, is a fine view, and wonderful colour effects in the evening.

Amrieh Station. This large village was formerly head of the Eastern district of the Western Desert Province, but the Administration is transferring to Burg el Arab. Bedouins come to the train, bigger and wirier than the Egyptians, and more graceful; they wear rough white robes and soft dark red tarbooshes.—There is a fine walk from Amrieh to Mex—the best day's tramp near Alexandria. The path leads north from the station, by the communal gardens, then makes for a ridge where limestone is quarried. View from the top over the western arm of Mariout. Take the causeway that crosses the lake and on the further bank turn to the right, finally crossing the coastal ridge to Dekhela (Section VI) and so to Mex by the sea shore.

Ikingi Mariout Station. (Ikingi is Turkish for "second.")—A good centre for the wild flowers of February and March. Go northward towards the lake, and keep to the lower ground; the local flora is one of the finest in the world.

Bahig Station. Centre for two fine expeditions—Abousir on the coast, and St. Menas inland.

ABOUSIR

The ruins of Abousir lie 5½ miles N.W. from Bahig station. They can be found without a guide (*see* map). There is a good road as far as Bahig village (¾ mile). Just above the village is a big quarry, worked in ancient times and very picturesque. A path crosses the ridge rather to the left of this quarry, after which the ruins are in sight all the way. The end of Mariout has to be crossed, so the expedition should not be made in winter on account of the mud. The last half hour of the journey is magnificent. The Temple and the Tower stand out on the height, which is golden with marigolds in spring time; and near the top of the ascent the sea appears through a gap, deep blue, and beating against a beach of snowy sand. The flowers can be amazing, colouring the earth in every direction. The ruins are supposed by the Bedouins to be the palace of Abou Zeit; they really mark the Ptolemaic city of Taposiris, whose name is preserved in the modern Abousir.

Taposiris must have been built soon after Alexandria (about 300 B.C.), and it is instructive to compare the two towns. They stand on the same spur—Taposiris at its base, where it has emerged from the mass of the desert. The lake is to their south, the sea to their north, so each commanded two harbours, to the advantage of their trade. Each has a lighthouse, each worshipped Osiris. Little is known of the history of Taposiris—called the "Great" to distinguish it from "Little" Taposiris at Montazah (p. 186). Its immediate trade was with the lake, its sea harbour being ½ mile below, at the vanished port of Plinthinus. The Arabs turned the Temple of Osiris into a fortress, and in modern times coast guards have been installed here.

The chief remains are:—

(i). *Temple of Osiris.* The eastern, and main, entrance adjoins the coast-guard station. At first sight it looks no more than a hole in a ruined wall, but it can easily be reconstructed. Each side of the entrance were Gate-towers (Pylons) like those of Edfu or Kom Ombo in Upper Egypt. Their bases project from the main wall, and up the face of each are two grooves for flag staffs, from whose tops crimson streamers floated. Staircases, reached from the inside, ascend each tower, and there are also two square rooms in the base of each.

The enclosure—about 100 yards square—is in a terrible mess. The actual temple has disappeared. There must have been a colonnaded court with an altar in the middle, and beyond it the temple façade: on north and south of temple would have been other courts. The arrangements were Egyptian, but some of the workmen were Greek; mason marks with Greek letters (*e.g.* Alpha Kappa Rho) have been found on the stone in the boundary wall.

The north boundary wall of the enclosure is very fine; it projects over the slope of the hill and rests on substructures: in it is a gate for the descent to the sea. Note the projections in the masonry. In the northwest corner are some architectural fragments, piled up by the Arabs.

(ii). *Lighthouse.* The ruined tower on the hill to the east of the temple was once mistaken for a tomb, since it stands in the ancient cemetery. It is really the Ptolemaic lighthouse of Taposiris, first of a chain that stretched from the Pharos at Alexandria all down the North African coast to Cyrene. It has, like the Pharos, three stages: a square basement, an octagonal central stage and a cylindrical top. On the north, where the

ABOUSIR AND DISTRICT

outer wall of the octagon has fallen, one can see the marks of the staircase by which the wood was carried to the top—a simpler version of the double spiral that ascended the huge Alexandrian building. There can be no doubt that the Taposiris lighthouse was modelled on its gigantic contemporary—scale about $\frac{1}{10}$th—and it is thus of great importance to archaeologists and historians (*see* p. 144 ff.).

There are tombs close to the lighthouse, and tombs and houses all along the slope to the south of the temple.

(iii). *Causeway.* South of the town, in the bed of the lake, are traces of the embankment that connected with the desert. It was doubtless pierced with arches like the Heptastadion at Alexandria, to allow boats to go through.

The other point of interest in the district is *Burg el Arab* (Modern Bahig). It lies some miles west of Bahig village (*see* above) but is easily located by the tower of the new carpet factory. Here is to be the capital of the Eastern District of the Western Desert Province Frontier Districts Administration; it is being planned and executed with great taste, thanks mainly to the genius of the Officer Commanding, W. E. Jennings Bramly, M.C. The factory consists of a great cloister and of two halls, one each side of the big tower. Fragments of antique sculpture and architecture have been cleverly introduced. The carpets are woven from camels' and goats' hair by Bedouin and Senussi women— the industry was started at Amrieh, during the late war. Specimens can be had in the Alexandrian shops. Further to the west other buildings are rising, including a small walled town. It is all most interesting, and one of the few pieces of modern creative work to be seen in these parts.

ST. MENAS

Seven and a half miles south of Bahig Station, in the loneliness of the desert, lie the ruins of a great Christian city. They can be visited between trains on a good horse, but it is better to camp out. The track passes over gently undulating expanses of limestone. The scenery grows less interesting, the flora scarcer, as the coast is left behind. At last the monotony is broken by the square hut where the excavators used to live. The ancient name of the place is preserved in the modern —Abumna.

Menas, a young Egyptian officer, was martyred during his service in Asia Minor because he would not abandon Christ (A.D. 296). When the army moved back into Egypt his friends brought his ashes with them, and at the entrance of the Libyan Desert a miracle took place: the camel that was carrying the burden refused to go further. The saint was buried and forgotten. But a shepherd observed that a sick lamb that crossed the spot became well. He tried successfully with another lamb. Then a sick princess was healed. The remains were exhumed, and a church built over the grave.

This church can still be traced. It is the Basilica of the Crypt (Plan I, p. 212) date 350, to which, at the end of the century, an immense extension was added by the Emperor Arcadius. What caused so rapid a growth? Water. There were springs in the limestone that have since dried up, and that must have had curative powers. Baths were built, some of them opening out of a church (Plan II). Little flasks, stamped with the saint's image, were filled from the sacred source by his tomb. The environs were irrigated,

houses, walls, cemeteries built, until in the pure air a sacred
city sprang up, where religion was combined with hygiene.
Nor did the saint only protect invalids. He was also the
patron of the caravans that passed by him from Alexandria
to the Wady Natrun, the Siwan Oasis, and Tripoli, and
so he is always seen between two camels, who crouch in
adoration because he guides them aright. By the 6th century he had become god of the Libyan Desert, then less
deserted than now, and his fame, like that of his predecessor Serapis, had travelled all round the Mediterranean, and
procured him worshippers as far as Rome and France.

Islam checked the cult. But as late as the year 1,000, an
Arab traveller saw the great double basilica still standing.
Lights burned in the shrine night and day, and there was
still left a little trickle of "the beautiful water of St. Menas
that drives away pain."

The site, entirely forgotten, was discovered in 1905. It
has been carefully excavated. Little more than the ground
plans of the buildings remain, but they are most interesting, and the marble decorations delightful.

The Sanctuary Group. This lies a little to the
south of the excavators' huts. Combined length, nearly
400 ft. In the centre is the original church covering the
tomb. To its east is the impressive addition of Arcadius; to its west a baptistery. On its north side a monastery. The best view of the group is from a mound
outside the baptistery. The general arrangement is
quite clear (Plan I, p. 212). Taken in detail:—

(i). *Church of Arcadius.* Length nearly 200 feet. A
cruciform basilica with a nave and two aisles, and
aisled transepts. Over the intersection was a dome, beneath which, now much ruined by its fall, is the High
Altar. Behind the altar are curved steps that supported
the ecclesiastical throne. Both altar and throne are in
a square enclosure where the priests and singers stood;
a narrow alley connects it with the nave. The eastern
apse has been used for burials.

CHURCH OF

High
Altar

ATRIUM

Stairs

ARCADIUS

Main Entrance

Stairs

Portico

Crypt

Stairs
Chapel

PRIMITIVE
CHURCH
water

HOSPICE

Sacred

course

Baptistery

Font

ST MENAS
PLAN I
The Sanctuary
Group
Subterranean work thus ‒‒‒‒‒‒‒‒

ST. MENAS

PLAN II — THE SACRED BATHS

Heating

Sacred water course

To HOSPICE and SANCTUARY →

Bath
Bath Bath
Heating
Bath

Cistern

Bath
CHURCH
Fount
Bath
Fount
Bath

← To more BATHS

The Nave is paved with white marble from the Greek archipelago. Green and purple marbles (verde antico and porphyry) were also used. From its south aisle, three doors open into a fine atrium. This was the principal approach to the church. The north aisle opens—at its east end—on to a staircase that ascended to the roof of the church; the other doors to the monks' apartments and hospice (*see* below). The west end of the nave is irregular, because the apse of the primitive church impinges.

(ii). *Primitive Church.* A small, three-aisled basilica, not well preserved, but with interesting crypt. The descent to this is by a marble staircase that starts in the Arcadian church, passes by a portico with a vaulted roof of brick, and then, after a little, turns to the south into an oblong subterranean chamber. Here, amid rich decorations, the ashes of the young saint once lay, in a tomb that was probably visible from the church above. A bas-relief of him was fixed to the south wall; the place for the marble slab can still be seen there. The ugly bas-relief in the Alexandria Museum (Room I) is a copy. Attached to the crypt is a chapel once vaulted with gold mosaic; the well in it was made by treasure-hunters.

On the west of the church runs the sacred water course from which the sanctuary derived its fame. It is a subterranean cistern, over 80 yards long; a shaft was sunk into it from the nave. Passing, as it did, so near to the saint's remains, it had special sanctity. The water was used to fill flasks, and also in the adjacent Baptistery.

(iii). *The Baptistery* is square without and octagonal within. In its centre, down steps, is the chief font, which had an over-flow canal; we do not know how it was filled. The floor was richly inlaid with serpentine, porphyry and other marbles. There was a dome. On its south side is an atrium. On its western exterior, niches for statues.

A Baptistery of this type—separate from the rest of the church—is common enough in the West. But in the East it is unique. Only at St. Menas, where water was so prominent in the worship, does it occur.

Immediately to the north of the Sanctuary Group are the *Monastery Buildings and Hospice,* a confused labyrinth. Best is a hall paved with marble and one supported by eight columns. It lies 40 yards due north from the gate of the Primitive Church. These buildings, together with the Sanctuary Group that they served, cover an area of over 40,000 square yards.

The Sacred Baths (Plan II). About 80 yards from the Monastery Buildings. Best located by the fine circular cistern of well-cut limestone blocks. The main building has a heating apparatus and three baths. Also a small but finely finished church; basilica type; apses at each end; three aisles. Two baths open straight out of its south aisles, and in its nave are two marble fountains that were probably filled from the source in the central sanctuary (*see* above). Throughout the arrangements are significant. The line between the hygienic and the miraculous is nowhere clearly drawn; heating apparatus and church have each to play their parts. Date of the group, probably 5th century. Another group lies beyond.

Northern Cemetery. This, the most important in the city, is some way from the groups above described. Indeed the visitor from Bahig leaves it to his left on his way to the hut. There is a good view of it from a mound. The main object is a church (150 ft. long), with three aisles, a square apse and numerous mortuary chapels where the more prominent invalids were buried. Others lie outside. Late date—7th–9th cent.

This by no means catalogues the ruins of St. Menas. There is a Southern Cemetery, private houses, wine presses, a kiln where the terra cotta flasks were made. All the desert around shows remains of the curious cult, which in some ways anticipated the methods of Lourdes.

Half a day over the desert southward brings a rider to the Wady Natrun.

THE WADY NATRUN

The Wady is best visited by arrangement with the Egyptian Salt and Soda Company, who have the concession for developing that section of it where the Lakes and the Monasteries lie. The Company's private railway starts at Khatatbeh, on the branch line between Cairo and Tel-el-Baroud (see Map, p. 187). The train curves up the desert to Bir Victoria, where it waters beneath a solitary tree. Then it leaves civilisation, and for three hours nothing is seen except an occasional gazelle. At the end of that time the ground falls away to the left, and the monastery of St. Macarius appears far off. Then is seen the chain of the lakes, and across them, often in mirage, the monasteries of St. Pschoi and The Syrians. The train descends to the terminus of Bir Hooker, close to the Company's factory and rest house.

The Wady Natrun (i.e. Natron, Soda) is a curious valley that begins near Cairo, and slopes northwestward into the heart of the Libyan Desert. It may have once been an outlet of the Nile, though it is barred now from the sea by coastal hills. Its upper and lower reaches are both barren, but in the central section—that which the railway taps—water survives in the form of a chain of mineral lakes.

The deposits were worked from antiquity, but with the rise of monasticism the Wady took a new importance, owing to its discomfort. As early as A.D. 150 St. Fronto retreated here from Alexandria. St. Ammon followed in 270; St. Macarius or Mercury a hundred years later. The more moderate ascetics extracted soda with the assistance of laymen; the extremists sought a waterless stretch called Scetis —probably the southern portion of the valley where the monastery to St. Macarius still stands. There were soon 5,000 monks. It is natural that so remote a community should lose touch with the theological niceties of the capital, and in 399 the Patriarch Theophilus was obliged to rebuke the monks for minimising the divine element in the Second Person. Their reply was startling. They crossed the desert, stormed Alexandria, and made the Patriarch apologise. A few years later he led an army into the Wady to punish them, but by now, oddly enough, they had veered to the opposite error; they minimised the human element. The truth is they represented native Egypt, the Patriarch the Hellenising coast (*see* p. 56). The quarrel was racial rather than theological, and when in the 6th century it came to a head, the Wady became the natural stronghold of the national or Monophysite party who, under the name of Copts, worship there to this day.

With the 19th century came a new colony—the industrial. It is the factory chimney of the Salt and Soda Company that now dominates the scene. The lakes are dredged for their deposits. The chief product is caustic soda which is poured red hot into metal drums, and exported all over the east. Ordinary soda (natron) is also produced. The factory is interesting. It, and the surrounding settlement, are due in their present form to Mr. A. H. Hooker, after whom the settlement is named.

More than eighty different species of birds have been identified in the marshes surrounding Bir Hooker.

The Mineral Lakes.

These lie between the factory and the monasteries.

THE NATRUN MONASTERIES

PLAN I - CHURCH OF ST. PSCHOI

Stucco Decoration

Altar

Sanctuary

doors

Choir

Semidome:
Death of
Virgin

Semidome.
Annunciation
and Nativity

Stone   screen

doors

Relics

Stone   Screen

Basin
○
for feet

Porch

Scale
├─────┤
10 feet

Semidome:
Ascension

→ To Refectory

THE NATRUN MONASTERIES – PLAN II
Convent of the Syrians – Church of the Virgin

Some of them are squalid, others are indescribably beautiful, especially in summer. The deposits form at the bottom. As they reach the top, the lake seems to be covered with white and crimson ice, in the midst of which are pools of blue and green water, and trickling streams of claret, and tracts that blush like a rose. When the scene is in mirage, its strangeness passes belief. A bird looks as big as a man, and the lump of salt it perches on shows like a boat of snow. The finest of these lakes is just to the left of Bir Hooker.

The Monasteries.

Four of these survive, and there are the ruins of many others. They are all of the same type, and to avoid repetitions it may be thus summarised:

Exterior:—an enclosure of stone laid in the middle of the desert, covering about an acre. Palm trees and buildings show over its walls. The walls are blank except for one high arch, which indicates the position of a little door, the only entrance. The black-robed monks, when the bell has been rung, look down from the parapet, then unbar the door, and take the traveller to the Guest House for coffee and lemonade. They are dirty and ignorant, but most courteous and hospitable. All payment is refused.

In the enclosure:—two or three churches, normally consisting of nave, choir, and sanctuary (kaikal). Refectory. Sleeping cells for the monks. Mill for grinding corn. Oven, where is baked the hard brown bread, and also the "isbodikon" (somatikon, sacrament), a cake of fine flour beautifully stamped with a cross and used for the Eucharist. Olive press. Granary. Garden of palm trees, bananas, capsicums, etc. Keep (kasr) for final retreat when attacked; reached only by a drawbridge from the parapet of the wall; contains library, dungeons, chapels; usually dedicated to St. Michael.

Date: general appearance and arrangement are of the 6th century. Most of the details are later.

Extract from the Thanksgiving offered at the arrival of a distinguished visitor:—

He who visits these mansions with firm faith, fervent desire, true repentance and good works, shall have all his sins forgiven. Then, O my reverend fathers and my beloved brethren, come that we may pray for these our dear and honourable brethren, who are come upon this visit and have reached these habitations, let us pray that Jesus Christ, who was with his servants in every time and every place, may now be with them, and may deliver them from all sins and iniquities. May he grant them the best of gifts and full reward, recompensing them for all that they have endured through toil and peril and the weariness of the journey as they travelled hither; giving them abundance of blessing; bring them back to their homes in safety; and after long life transport them to the brightness of Paradise and the life of bliss, through the intercession of Our Lady the Virgin, and of all our holy fathers. Amen.*

THE FOUR MONASTERIES.

(A). *Convent of St. Pschoi* (Deir Abou Bishoi).— About an hour's ride from Bir Hooker. Dedicated to St. Pschoi or Besa. "B" is the Coptic article, so the saint's name is ultimately "Isa" *i.e.* Isaiah. Little is known about him.

The convent enclosure contains:

(i). *The Church of St. Pschoi* (Plan I, p. 218). 6th–11th cents. with later additions. A spacious entrance

* From A. J. Butler's Ancient Coptic Churches.

porch leads to the dark but impressive interior. There are three divisions: Nave, Choir and Sanctuary.

The Nave has an arched vault; massive piers with pointed arches divide it from its aisles. In it is an Ambon (lectern for reading the Gospel), and a small marble basin level with the floor, where the priest washes the feet of the people on Maundy Thursday in commemoration of the action of Christ. Many of the Nave arches have been blocked up to strengthen the building. High and narrow folding doors—recalling a Japanese screen—close the lofty arch that leads from the Nave into the Choir; they are set with fine carved panels, enclosed in ivory borders. Other doors lead from the aisles.

The Choir too has vaulting, but it is at right angles to that of the Nave. At each side of the Choir are chapels, probably of later date. Left—Chapel of the Virgin, with a chest containing the relics of St. Pschoi, whom the monks state remains intact. Right—Chapel of St. Ischyrion; off it is the Baptistery. The entrance into the Sanctuary is through ancient carved doors; over them is a triumphant arch.

The Sanctuary has, behind the altar, a fine tribune of six steps—three straight and three curved. In the centre was the throne of the Abbot. It has gone, and the marble decorations of the steps are ruined. Above the throne is a marble mosaic. In the centre of the eastern dome is a Cross.

(ii). *The Refectory.* This solemn room contains the immense stone table, narrow and low, at which the monks break their yearly fast. They do not eat here usually, and use the table as a drying place for onions, bread, etc., while cakes of salt are stacked against the wall. At the head of the table is the Abbot's seat. The place is rough and indescribably untidy. But one could scarcely find a more striking relic of primitive Christianity.

(B). *Convent of the Syrians* (Deir es Suriani).—
Close to the Convent of St. Pschoi. Founded by monks
from Syria. Dedicated to the Virgin. Here Robert Curzon (1833) discovered in the oil cellar priceless Syrian,
Coptic, and Abyssinian MSS., now in the British Museum. He describes his find in "Monasteries of the
Levant": it was facilitated by plying the Abbot with
liqueurs. More were brought away by Archdeacon Tattam, and nothing valuable remains now.

The enclosure contains:—

(i). *Church of the Virgin* (Plan II, p. 219). A fine
building 40 ft. by 90, probably the model for the church
in St. Pschoi—*i.e.* originating in the 6th century.

The Nave has piers with high pointed arches, and
lofty vaulting, slightly pointed. In the middle, the basin for the Maundy feet washing, a marble slab with a
circular depression. In the western semi-dome, fine
fresco of the Ascension. Precious folding doors between
nave and choir, inlaid with ivory panels of Christ in
the nimbus of the Cross, the Virgin, St. Peter and St.
Mark; round their posts and lintels a Syriac inscription,
dating them back to the 7th century.

The Choir—North semi-dome; fresco of the Death of
the Virgin. South semi-dome; fresco of the Annunciation and Nativity. Admirable work. More ancient doors
between Choir and Sanctuary; ivory panel representing Dioscurus (Patriarch of Alexandria 450 and founder
of Monophysism, *see* p. 56), Mark, Emmanuel, the Virgin, Ignatius, and Severus (512). Syriac inscriptions of
rather later type—8th century.

Sanctuary—Skilful and effective plaster frieze with
a border below and panels of conventional trees and
vines above. Above the eastern niche a panel of

crosses. This unique decoration should be studied closely.

(ii). *Smaller Church of the Virgin.* Over its entrance to the southwest a marble cross in low relief. Inside, another cross in black marble. Probably dedication crosses. Pulpit in the choir.

(iii). *Tamarind tree under the enclosing wall.* St. Ephraim the Syrian (date 373) inadvertently, so they say, laid his staff down, and it took root at once. But it is unlikely that St. Ephraim ever visited Egypt.

(C). *Convent of St. Baramus* (Deir el Baramus).— About two hours ride from Bir Hooker. Dedicated to an unknown saint (Romaios ?).

In the enclosure are:—

(i). *Church of the Virgin.* The piers of the nave are built round antique marble columns. There are ten dedication crosses, marking places signed with holy oil at the consecration of the church—six in the nave and four in the choir. Fine carvings on the sanctuary screen. In the reliquary lie the brothers SS. Maximus and Domitius from whose mouths, when they prayed, fiery ropes ascended to Heaven. Attached to this church are two smaller ones—St. George (Mari Girgis) now used as a granary; it has an ornamented dome— and St. Theodore (Al Amir Tadrus).

(ii). *Church of Baramus.*—Ruined by restoration.

(iii). *The Refectory.*—Similar to that at St. Pschoi. Date 5th or 6th century. At this entrance is a great book-rest of stone.

(iv). *Keep.*—With chapel to St. Michael.

(D). *Convent of St. Macarius* (Deir Abou Makar).—This monastery is the least accessible of the four, being ten miles from Bir Hooker.

St. Macarius, or Mercury, the founder, was an Alex-

andrian who was seen by another saint in a vision kill-
ing the apostate Emperor Julian (d. 363). He is also
celebrated for a bunch of grapes that he refused to eat,
and for a mosquito that he killed. Overcome with remorse at its death, he retired naked to the marshes
near, and at the end of six months was so distended
by stings that the brethren could only recognise him
by his voice. He selected this site for his monastery on
account of the badness of the communications and
water supply. It was repaired in 880. Of its later history
nothing is known.

The monastery enclosure is on the usual plan. It
contains:—

(i). *Church of Macarius.* Byzantine in character;
three sanctuaries, a choir, and an irregular western
end. The central sanctuary is roofed by a fine brick
dome, once covered with frescoes, and still showing
traces of its ancient windows, with their stucco parti-
tions and tiny panels of coloured glass. There were also
frescoes in the eastern niche, and paintings upon the
entrance arch. The sanctuary doors are well carved.

Left of Sanctuary: Chapel of St. John, with a double
screen. The outer screen is set with exquisitely carved
panels—probably 8th century. Frame later. The plaster
of the dome has fallen; it too was once coloured. St.
Macarius lies in the Reliquary.

(ii). *Church of the Elders* (Al Shiulah).—Marked by
a detached bell-tower. A small building of similar plan.
One of its columns has a late classical capital.

(iii). *Church of St. Ischyrion* (Abou Iskharun).—One
of the martyrs whom Alexandria, in the past, so freely
produced. A magnificent low-pitched dome almost
covers both choir and nave. It is made of bricks that
must have been carried on camels from the Delta.

(iv). *The Keep* (Kasr).—Reached by a flight of steps

and a drawbridge. On its first floor are three chapels dedicated to:—

St. Michael—Corinthian and Doric capitals in the nave; the Sanctuary Screen has ivory inlay; in the Sanctuary are the bodies of sixteen patriarchs, each in a plain deal box: St. Anthony—three ancient frescoed figures: and St. Suah, with more frescoes. On the ground floor, a chapel to the Virgin, with a triple altar containing depressions of unknown use.

THE MODERN RELIGIOUS COMMUNITIES

The ecclesiastical life of Alexandria is not as intense to-day as in the days of St. Athanasius, but it is even more complicated. The city is the seat of four patriarchates, and many other religious bodies are represented in her. The complications are partly due to the activity of Roman Catholicism, which, in order to win oriental schismatics back to the fold, has in each case created a counter church that shall approximate as nearly as possible to the conditions and ritual that are familiar—e.g. an Armenian Catholic Church for the Armenians, a Coptic Catholic for the Copts. And further complications proceed from the modern commercial communities who tend to regard religion as an expression of nationality rather than of dogma.

The following list of the Churches may indicate the unsuspected vastness of the subject:—

GREEK PATRIARCHATE: "Orthodox Greek," or "Melchite" church (from Melek, Arabic for King). Present Patriarch, Photius I. His position is curious. He is a subject neither to the Kingdom of Greece, nor to the Patriarch of Constantinople, but holds, or rather held, his position from the Sultan of Turkey direct. Thus ecclesiastically he is independent. His title is "Patriarch of Alexandria, Libya, Pentapolis, Ethiopia, and all Egypt," but his patriarchate does not extend beyond Egypt, which he administers through four bishops. Historically he represents the church that kept loyal to Byzantium and to the Emperor at the Council of Chalcedon (A.D. 451) when the rest of Egypt began to drift away over the Monophysite question. After the Arab Conquest the Greek Patriarch resided in Cairo, but came back to Alexandria about sixty years ago to the Convent and Church of St. Saba (p. 114). As for dogma, the Greek Orthodox chiefly differs from the Roman Catholic and the Protestants over the "Filioque" clause in the Nicene creed. It holds that the Holy Ghost proceeded not from the Father and the Son, but through the Son. This is the point over which the East and West split, and failed to reunite in 1459.

CHURCHES OF THE GREEK COMMUNITY: These too are Greek Orthodox in faith. But they do not recognise the Patriarch. Indeed their relations with him during the late war were of the liveliest. They are the churches of a body of business men who only owe allegiance to the Kingdom of Greece. They are self-administering, and choose their own priests. The Patriarch, however, has the right of examining those priests' credentials, and of giving them permission to officiate. The Community has a Cathedral (The Annunciation) near the Place St. Catherine (p. 154); also three churches in Ramleh,—St. Stefano, St. Nicolas, and the Prophet Elias.

SYRIAN GREEK ORTHODOX: The Church of those members of the Syrian Community who hold the Greek Orthodox faith. Independent of the Patriarch. Under an archimandrite. Services in Arabic. Church—"Dormition de la Sainte Vierge" in the Rue el Kaid Gohar.

This completes the Greek Orthodox Churches.

COPTIC PATRIARCHATE: The Copts are Monophysites— i.e. believe that after the Incarnation the Divine and the Human in Christ were united into a single nature (p. 81). This severs them from the rest of Christendom. Histori-

cally the Patriarchate is the opponent of the Greek Orthodox Patriarchate, from whom it split at the Council of
Chalcedon, and it claims to represent Egyptian Christianity. In 960 the Patriarch went to reside at Cairo, and the
custom has continued, though the title of "Patriarch of
Alexandria" was retained. Besides his powers in Egypt, the
Patriarch consecrates the Metropolitan of Abyssinia. Alexandria has a resident archbishop. Cathedral—in the Rue de
l'Eglise Copte (p. 175).

ARMENIAN CHURCH: Founded by St. Gregory the Illu-
minator in the 4th century, and, like the Coptic, Monophysite. Its head is a "Catholicos" at Etchmiadzin, Armenia.
The Alexandrian community has a church, SS. Peter and
Paul, Rue Abou el Dardaa (p. 156).

We now come to the group of churches that are in communion with Rome. Dogma, identical. Rite, differing.

LATIN PATRIARCHATE: Founded after the Crusades—13th
century. The Patriarch does not reside but lives at Rome,
and governs through an Apostolic Vicar who lives at Alexandria. Chief Church—Cathedral of St. Catherine (Place
St. Catherine, p. 155).

COPTIC PATRIARCHATE: Organised in 1895, with title of
"Patriarchate of Alexandria and of all the Preaching of St.
Mark." The Patriarch resides at Alexandria, and adminis-
ters Egypt through the suffragan bishops of Hermopolis
Magna and Thebes. Cathedral—Rue de l'Hôpital Indigène
(p. 169).

GREEK CATHOLIC CHURCH: Under the Patriarch of Antioch who now lives at Damascus and governs Alexandria
through a Vicar General. Church: St. Pierre, Rue Debbane
(p. 174). The priests generally officiate in Arabic, though
the ecclesiastical language is Greek.

MARONITE CHURCH: Founded in the 5th century by St.
Maro, and at one time adhering to the Monothelite heresy.

This was a fainter version of the Monophysite, and asserted that though Christ might have two natures, He only had one will (p. 82). The Catholic view is that Christ had two wills, human and divine, which were exercised in unison, and in the 18th century the Maronite Community subscribed to this, and is consequently in communion with Rome. Patriarch at Antioch. Ecclesiastical language—Syrian. Church at Alexandria in the Rue de l'Eglise Maronite (p. 153).

ARMENIAN CATHOLIC CHURCH: Under the Patriarchate of Cilicia, formed in the 18th century. There is a Bishop of Alexandria, but he lives at Cairo. Church—Rue Averoff (p. 175).

CHALDEAN CATHOLIC CHURCH: Under the Patriarchate of Babylon, formed 1843, to counteract the Nestorian heresy. The Chaldeans of Alexandria, 100 strong, are said to be looking for a plot of ground on which to build a church.

This concludes the Catholic group. As regards the Protestants:

UNITED PRESBYTERIAN CHURCH OF EGYPT: Most, but not all, native Protestants belong to this body. It is attached to the American Mission, which proselytizes mainly among the Copts. Church—Rue Tewfik I.

CHURCH OF ENGLAND: Alexandria is in the diocese of Egypt and the Sudan. The official church of the British community is St. Marks in the Square, built on land given to the community by Mohammed Ali (p. 110). There is another Anglican church at Ramleh (All Saints) built by some residents there. Its living, after some heart-burnings, has been placed in the hands of the Bishop of London (p. 181).

CHURCH OF SCOTLAND: St. Andrew's, in the French Gardens.

APPENDIX II

THE DEATH OF CLEOPATRA
(p. 30)

The death of Cleopatra as described by Plutarch took hold of the imagination of posterity, and was dramatised by Shakespeare and by Dryden.

(i). PLUTARCH (in North's Translation which Shakespeare used).

Her death was very sodain. For those whom Caesar sent unto her ran thither in all haste possible, and found the soldiers standing at the gate, mistrusting nothing, nor understanding of her death. But when they had opened the doors, they found Cleopatra stark dead, laid upon a bed of gold, attired and arrayed in her royal robes, and one of her two women, which was called Iras, dead at her feet: and her other woman called Charmian half dead, and trembling, trimming the diadem which Cleopatra wore upon her head. One of the soldiers seeing her, angrily said to her: Is that well done, Charmian? Very well said she again, and meet for a princess descended of so many royal kings. She said no more, but fell down dead hard by the bed.

(ii). SHAKESPEARE (Antony and Cleopatra, Act V, Scene 2).

Cleopatra. Give me my robe, put on my crown; I have
Immortal longings in me; now no more
The juice of Egypt's grape shall moist this lip.
Yare, yare, good Iras; quick. Methinks I hear
Antony call; I see him rouse himself
To praise my noble act; I hear him mock
The luck of Caesar, which the gods give men
To excuse their after wrath: husband, I come:

Now to that name my courage prove my title!
I am fire and air; my other elements
I give to baser life. So; have you done?
Come then, and take the last warmth of my lips.
Farewell, kind Charmian; Iras, long farewell.

(kisses them. Iras falls and dies).

Have I the aspic in my lips? Dost fall?
If thou and nature can so gently part,
The stroke of death is as a lover's pinch,
Which hurts and is desired. Dost thou lie still?
If thus thou vanishest, thou tell'st the world
It is not worth leave-taking.

   Charmian. Dissolve thick cloud and rain; that I may say
The gods themselves do weep.

   Cleopatra.   This proves me base:
If she meet first the curled Antony
He'll make demand of her, and spend that kiss
Which is my heaven to have. Come thou mortal wretch

(to the asp, which she applies to her breast)

With thy sharp teeth this knot intrinsicate
Of life at once untie; poor venomous fool,
Be angry, and despatch. O! couldst thou speak,
That I might hear thee call great Caesar ass
Unpolicied.

   Charmian.   O eastern star!

   Cleopatra.   Peace, peace!
Dost thou not see my baby at my breast,
That sucks the nurse asleep?

   Charmian.   O, break! O, break!

   Cleopatra. As sweet as balm, as soft as air, as gentle—
O Antony!—Nay, I will take thee too.

(applying another asp to her arm)

What should I stay—   (dies).

   Charmian. In this vile world? So, fare thee well.
Now boast thee, death, in thy possession lies
A lass unparallel'd. Downy windows, close;
And golden Phœbus never be beheld
Of eyes again so royal! Your crown's awry;

I'll mend it, and then play.

                      (enter the Guard, rushing in)

First Guard. Where is the queen?

Charmian.   Speak softly, wake her not.

First Guard. Caesar hath sent—

Charmian.   Too slow a messenger.

                      (applies an asp)

O! come apace, dispatch; I partly feel thee.

First Guard. Approach, ho! All's not well; Caesar's be-
guil'd.

Second Guard. There's Dolabella sent from Caesar; call
him.

First Guard. What work is this? Charmian, is this well
done?

Charmian. It is well done and fitting for a princess
Descended of so many royal kings.

Ah! Soldier.   (dies)

(iii). DRYDEN (All for Love, Act V, Scene I).

Charmian.   To what end
These ensigns of your Pomp and Royalty?

Cleopatra. Dull that thou art! why, 'tis to meet my Love;
As when I saw him first, on Cydno's bank,
All sparkling, like a goddess; so adorned,
I'll find him, once again: my second spousals
Shall match my first in glory. Haste; haste, both,
And dress the bride of Antony.

Charmian.   'Tis done.

Cleopatra. Now set me by my lord. I claim this place:
For I must conquer Caesar too, like him,
And win my share o' th' world. Hail, you dear relics
Of my immortal love!

O let no impious hand remove you hence;
But rest for ever here. Let Egypt give
His death that peace, which it denied his life.
Reach me the casket.

Iras.   Underneath the fruit
The aspic lies.

               Welcome, thou kind deceiver!

Cleopatra.

                              (putting aside the leaves)
Thou best of thieves; who, with an easy key,
Dost open life, and, unperceived by us,
Ev'n steal us from ourselves; discharging so
Death's dreadful office, better than himself,
Touching our limbs so gently into slumber,
That Death stands by, deceived by his own image,
And thinks himself but sleep.

 Serapion (within).   The Queen, where is she?
The town is yielded, Caesar's at the gates.

 Cleopatra. He comes too late t'invade the rights of death.
Haste, bare my arm, and rouse the serpent's fury.

                    (holds out her arm, and draws it back)
Coward flesh—
Would'st thou conspire with Caesar to betray me,
As thou wert none of mine? I'll force thee to it
And not be sent by him,
But bring myself my soul to Antony.

                    (turns aside, and then shows her arm bloody)
Take hence; the work is done.

 Serapion (within)   Break ope the door
And guard the traitor well.

 Charmian.   The next is ours.

 Iras. Now, Charmian, be too worthy
Of our great queen and mistress.

                              (they apply the aspics)
 Cleopatra. Already, death, I feel thee in my veins;
I go with such a will to find my lord,
That we shall quickly meet.
A heavy numbness creeps through every limb,
And now 'tis at my head: my eyelids fall
And my dear love is vanished in a mist.
Where shall I find him, where? O turn me to him,
And lay me on his breast—Caesar, thy worst;
Now part us if thou canst.

                    (Dies. Iras sinks down at her feet and dies;
                    Charmian stands behind her chair as dress-
                    ing her head. Enter Serapion, two priests,
                    Alexas bound, Egyptians).

Two Priests. Behold, Serapion, what havoc death hath made.

Serapion. 'Twas what I feared. Charmian, is this well done?

Charmian. Yes, 'tis well done, and like a queen, the last Of her great race: I follow her.

(sinks down; dies).

APPENDIX III

THE UNCANONICAL GOSPELS OF EGYPT
(p. 77)

(i). FROM THE GOSPEL ACCORDING TO THE EGYPTIANS.

The Lord said unto Salome, who asked how long death would prevail, "As long as ye women bear children. I have come to undo the work of woman." And Salome said "Then have I done well in that I have not borne children." The Lord answered and said "Eat every plant, but that which has bitterness eat not." When Salome asked when would be known the things about which he spake (*i.e.* the Last Judgement) the Lord said "Whenever ye put off the garment of shame, when the two become one, and the male with the female, there being neither male nor female."

(ii). FROM THE GOSPEL ACCORDING TO THE HEBREWS.

Jesus saith:—"Let not him who seeks cease until he find and when he finds he shall be astonished; astonished, he shall reach the Kingdom, and having reached the Kingdom he shall rest."

(iii). FROM UNCERTAIN SOURCES (about 200 A.D.)

Jesus saith:—"Except ye fast to the world, ye shall in no wise find the Kingdom of God; and except ye make the sabbath a real sabbath, ye shall not see the Father."

Jesus saith:—"Wherever there are two, they are not

without God, and when ever there is one alone, I say, I am
with him. Raise the stone and there thou shalt find me;
cleave the wood, and there am I."

APPENDIX IV

THE NICENE CREED
(pp. 53 and 80)

Here is the text as originally passed by the Council, including the paragraph against the Arians; additions to the
original texts are enclosed within brackets.

We believe in one God, the Father Almighty, maker of
all things, both visible and invisible.

And in one Lord, Jesus Christ, the Son of God, begotten of the Father (only begotten, that is to say of the substance of the Father) God of God and Light of Light, very
God of very God, begotten, not made, being of one substance with the Father, by whom all things were made
(both things in Heaven and things on Earth); who for us
men and for our salvation came down and was made flesh,
made man, suffered and rose again on the third day, went
up into the heavens and is to come again to judge the
quick and the dead;

And in the Holy Ghost;

But the Holy Catholic and Apostolic Church anathe-
matises those who say that there was a time when the Son
of God was not, and that he was not before he was begotten, and that he was made from that which did not exist;
or who assert that he is of other substance or essence than
the Father, or is susceptible of change.

INDEX

DOLPHIN BOOKS AND DOLPHIN MASTERS

The bold face M indicates a Dolphin Master. Dolphin Masters are Dolphin Books in the editions of greatest importance to the teacher and student. In selecting the Dolphin Masters, the editors have taken particular pains to choose copies of the most significant edition (usually the first) by obtaining original books or their facsimiles or by having reproductions made of library copies of particularly rare editions. Facsimiles of original title pages and other appropriate material from the first edition are included in many Masters.

FICTION

POETRY AND DRAMA

HISTORY AND BIOGRAPHY

PHILOSOPHY AND RELIGION

ESSAYS AND LETTERS

MYSTERY